Kelly – It's great to work with you + Visit Rogers to attract visitors to our city.

Jm CMuy 2015

It All Starts Here

**CELEBRATING 125 YEARS AS THE COMPANY THAT TEACHES AMERICA TO SHOOT
1886 - 2011**

Joe C. Murfin

Daisy Outdoor Products
Rogers, Arkansas

Copyright © 2011 by Daisy Outdoor Products

All rights reserved. No part of this book may be reproduced or transmitted in any form whatsoever, by any means, electronic or mechanical, including photograph, photocopy, facsimile (fax), mimeograph, recording or any information storage and retrieval system, without prior written permission of the Publisher, excepting brief quotes used in connection with reviews written specifically for inclusion in publication or broadcast.

ISBN 978-0-9830772-1-3

Printed in Rogers, Arkansas, U.S.A.
First Printing 2011

Daisy Outdoor Products

Daisy Outdoor Products
P.O. Box 220
Rogers, Arkansas 72757
www.daisy.com

SPECIAL THANKS

Writing this book was anything but a lone venture. My most effective research involved prying into the amazing memories of some of the finest Daisy story tellers.

I'd like to single out just a few of the people who made this project possible.

Cass Hough
The book *It's a Daisy!* was published in much the same fashion as was this book. Both Cass and I, while employed by Daisy, wrote books on the occasion of significant anniversary dates for the purpose of preserving the history of a company which we hold dear. Although the books differ in format and style, I like to think the two volumes are now a set; both required reading for anyone wishing to know the personality, heart and corporate culture of this great old company.

Dick Daniel, John Ford and Orin Ribar
Among the many who contributed details which are woven into these chapters, these three possess a wealth of experience and detailed knowledge of Daisy, its history, programs and products. Most amazingly, they cited names, dates and places that bring these stories to life.

Jim Langford
Jim has worked on Daisy graphics for so long that he was a natural choice to handle the design and production of this book. Jim knows Daisy's style, and I sense this project became as much a labor of love for him as it was for me.

Ross Murfin and Debbie Murfin
My older brother and my wife, both of whom I deeply respect. One a professor, college administrator, author, and editor, the other a loving friend and partner, they equally understood the significance of this project to Daisy and to me. I've admired and loved them for 59 and 31 years, respectively.

Ray Hobbs, Bruce Wolf, Drew Albright and Kyle Werst
Thanks to the current Daisy management team for allowing me to devote a significant number of days to this project and for appreciating its importance. It would have been a shame to let the recent history of Daisy, our accomplishments, escape without being captured in this book. Without Ray's interest and permission and the support and participation of the rest of the management team, this book would have never been published.

Contents

Special Thanks		*iii*
Foreword		*1*
Chapter 1	Setting the Record Straight	3
Chapter 2	Historical Significance	10
Chapter 3	What's in the Box?	20
Chapter 4	BBs and Ball Bearings	26
Chapter 5	Ralphie Got it Wrong	32
Chapter 6	The Daisy Family	36
Chapter 7	At Home in Rogers	46
Chapter 8	Teaching America to Shoot	56
Chapter 9	Defending What's Right	68
Chapter 10	A Museum With a History	76
Chapter 11	Are We Home Yet?	90
Chapter 12	Once Every 120 Years	95
Chapter 13	Thinking Outside the Daisy Box	100
Chapter 14	It All Starts Here	112
Postscript		*122*
Acknowledgments		*124*

Foreword
Standing on Strong Shoulders

It was 1976 when Cass Hough's book *It's a Daisy!* was first published by Daisy and 2006 when a thirtieth anniversary edition was re-printed. Cass Hough obviously held the credentials to write the consummate book on Daisy history. His grandfather, Lewis Cass Hough, had test fired the first "Daisy" in his office. His father Edward Hough joined the company in 1893 and Cass came on board in 1926. From the beginning, and for many years to come, Daisy was a family company.

There are those who would challenge some of the colorful legends and anecdotes perpetuated in Cass's book. However, official records are too often limited to boardroom motions and key business decisions and lack detail regarding day to day operations. History is equally wary of and wise to rely on stories handed down from one generation to the next. We, who consider ourselves a part of the Daisy Family today, are grateful to the Hough family for preserving that history which might, otherwise, have gone unrecorded.

This book is not intended to be a sequel to *It's a Daisy!*. It is, however, written with a sense of obligation not to let the written history of this amazing company end in 1976. I am humbled by the opportunity not simply to pick up where Cass left off but to bring into perspective what it means to work for a company which has flourished in business for 125 years. The recipe for this book, like that of *It's a Daisy!*, includes cold hard corporate records blended with a measure of personal insight from those who participated in this company's numerous successes.

In this book we will celebrate the Daisy brand, locations and programs. None of these subjects, however, has been the key to Daisy's success. On the occasion of Daisy's 125th Anniversary (even that number sparks controversy) we, the current Daisy Family, stand on strong shoulders of two groups of people who have brought this great company to this particular point in American business history. We dedicate this book to the generations of loyal Daisy customers who haven't just purchased our product but who have truly loved it. And, we dedicate this book to our Daisy Family, those innovative and hard working individuals who have set the stage for this company's continued success.

First   The name of this Corporation shall be the "Plymouth Iron Wind Mill Company."

Second   The Capital Stock of the Corporation shall be Fifty Thousand Dollars ($50000.—) divided into five hundred (500) shares of One Hundred Dollars ($100.—) each.

Third   This Corporation is formed for the purpose of manufacturing the "Hamilton" Iron Wind-Mill and of manufacturing such other articles as the Board of Directors shall from time to time direct.

Fourth   The term of the existence of this Corporation shall be Thirty Years.

Fifth   The names of the Stockholders, their respective residences, and the number of shares held by each are as follows:

Sixth   The business & affairs of this Corporation shall be managed by a Board of Directors consisting of Seven persons, who shall be chosen annually by the Stockholders from their number and shall hold their offices for the term of one year and until their successors are chosen.
         The Directors shall choose one of their number as President, and shall also choose a Secretary and Treasurer as the By-Laws of the Corporation shall permit.

CHAPTER 1
SETTING THE RECORD STRAIGHT

When a company has survived 125 years, it's highly likely there has been a fire which has destroyed, or an acquisition which has purged, its historical records. Daisy is fortunate not to fall into either category. Rather, the company has operated free of disaster which might have destroyed the early Board of Directors' books of minutes, old letters and documentation of annual sales which the company has had the honor of safekeeping since the 1880s. Additionally, three generations of Hough family leadership helped to ensure a seamless transition not only of management but also of corporate lore and anecdotal history.

There are several colorful stories in Daisy's history which challenge the imagination of some collectors and historians. For the purposes of this book, Daisy continues to promulgate their factuality. Some say that if these stories were true they would have been recorded in early board books. Daisy would argue that such trivial details related to the day to day operation of a business are rarely brought to the attention of a company's directors and more rarely appear in the pages of board minutes.

A Daisy of a Name

In the late 1870s Clarence Hamilton, a watchmaker and inventor by trade, moved from Ohio to Plymouth, Michigan. There he set up shop in the front window of R.L. Root's drug and jewelry store on Main Street, where he repaired watches. He designed and patented a metal vaneless windmill and began production in a shop near his home about 1880. In 1882 a group of Plymouth businessmen invested thirty thousand dollars, purchased twenty-five acres of land in the heart of Plymouth for $400, built a two-story, 8,000 square foot building, formed the Plymouth Iron Windmill Company and began production of the windmills.

By the mid 1880s business was dropping off. There was no real means of advertising beyond word of mouth, and transporting the heavy steel windmill by wagon throughout the southern part of Michigan, northern Indiana and Ohio was difficult. In January 1888 the board met to consider closing the company. The motion to liquidate failed by one vote, that of general manager Lewis Cass Hough.

At a meeting of the Directors of the Plymouth Iron Windmill Co. held at the office of L.C.Hough & Son on Jan 26th 1895. Directors present. H.W. Baker, T.C. Sherwood, L.C. Hough & J. Hamilton.

The following resolution was offered by T.C. Sherwood and unanimously adopted.

Resolved, that the name Plymouth Iron Windmill Company be changed to the Daisy Manufacturing Company and that certificate of such change be filed with the secretary of State as required by law.

No further business, adjourned.

C.C. Hough, Sec'y

At a meeting of the Directors of the Daisy Mfg. Co. held at the office of L.C.Hough & Son on Feb. 19th it was moved and supported that the Company declare a dividend of 10% on all stock. Carried.

C.C. Hough, Sec'y

Around the corner from the windmill company, Hamilton had purchased a livery stable. There he operated the Plymouth Air Rifle Company, producing a wooden airgun to compete with the one being manufactured by the Markham Air Rifle Company. Within a matter of months, Hamilton was matching Markham's production of a hundred guns a day. Because everything in the late 1800s was hand-built, one hundred guns a day was a significant production number.

On March 6, 1888, Hamilton approached the windmill company with an all-metal airgun of his own design. He chose to take it to the windmill company because they had blast furnaces and they were equipped to mold and stamp the metal parts necessary to build his gun. The gun was passed around to members of the board. General Manager L.C. Hough test fired the gun and exclaimed, "Boy, that's a Daisy." ("It's a Daisy" was a colloquialism of the time.) So the little gun was named, Daisy.

Legend has it that the board of the Plymouth Iron Windmill Company decided to build the gun and offer it as a premium item to every farmer who purchased a windmill. In a speech made to Rotarians in Plymouth, Michigan, Charles Bennett, L.C. Hough's nephew who had joined the windmill company as a salesman January 9, 1890, related the early history of the Windmill Company and Daisy.

According to Mr. Bennett, he began buying the BB guns and carrying them around with him, selling them to the farm boys when he made a call to sell windmills. He bought the guns from the company for seventy-five cents and found he could sell them for $2.00. Many times, while out with his horse and buggy selling windmills, he would sell the farmer a gun for his boy for only one dollar but take the other dollar out in lodging for himself and his horse for Saturday and Sunday. Considering the fact that Bennett was empowered to be flexible in his price and often discounted the gun to secure lodging or close the windmill sale, it is quite believable that he might have given away some Daisy guns in order to sell windmills.

Courtesy of the Plymouth Historical Museum, Plymouth, MI

The gun was cocked by pulling up on the rear sight and loaded by simply dropping a BB down the muzzle. The board of the windmill company voted to "...build the gun for one year or as long as the money lasted." If they ran out of money before that time, they were going to close the plant down.

By 1895 the sales and popularity of the gun had grown to the point that the company ceased the manufacture of windmills, began producing airguns exclusively and changed its name to Daisy Manufacturing Company.

Since 1886

The slogan "Since 1886" has probably been used more often by Daisy than any other. If the windmill company was founded in 1882 and the first Daisy BB gun was patented in 1889, how does Daisy trace its history to 1886?

The Markham Manufacturing Company of Plymouth, Michigan, was, in 1885, initially in the business of manufacturing wooden water buckets, tanks and cisterns. The Markham Air Rifle Company was established in July 1886 in a small two-story factory, the first ever built solely for the manufacture of air rifles. The building was located on Main Street, across the Pere Marquette Railroad tracks from the Plymouth Iron Windmill Company property.

W. F. (Phil) Markham, President of the Markham Air Rifle Company, a Plymouth native, born January 22, 1851, was a very successful and colorful citizen of downtown Plymouth. He purchased a large boat that he kept on an area lake and often wore a captain's hat, referring to himself as "Captain" Markham. He may be best known for the impressive three-story mansion with an enclosed park, pool and deer run which he built, downtown, across from his former home.

Although Markham has been given credit for the invention of the first commercially successful BB gun, research indicates it is more likely that he was the gun's promoter and that George W. Sage was the gun's designer. While the principles of spring air rifle design were well known and had been used in the manufacture of workable rifles for centuries, the combination of inexpensive materials, reduced velocity and an easy cocking mechanism made the Markham Chicago model the first financially successful BB gun.

Mr. Markham's request to secure financing for his company was denied by the Plymouth city fathers. However, a local businessman, Elmer Chaffee, sold half of his grocery business and went into partnership with Mr. Markham. He became secretary-treasurer and ten percent shareholder. Elmer Chaffee hired his younger brother, A.W. (Alfred) to be the company's first salesman. On Alfred's first sales trip to Chicago, he secured a sizeable order from the Strobel and Wilken Company with the stipulations that the gun not be sold to any other wholesaler in Chicago and that the gun be renamed the Chicago Air Rifle.

In 1899 one of Chaffee's retail customers requested a metal air rifle. Markham wasn't equipped to produce that gun so Chaffee approached Daisy. In 1900 Daisy produced the Number 4 and Number 5 Sentinel guns for Mr. Chaffee. Chaffee would later serve on Daisy's board of directors.

When he decided to leave Plymouth, Markham contacted Daisy executives E.C. Hough and Charlie Bennett and sold them his airgun company on December 31, 1912. Hough and Bennett changed the name of the company to King Manufacturing Company in 1928.

Mr. Markham relocated to Hollywood, California, and bought the vacant southwest corner of Sunset Boulevard and Vine Street, where he built the "Morning Gate Villa" estate (the 1920 Census indicates the location to be 1413 Vine Street). He was one of Hollywood's early developers and built the Markham Building at the southwest corner of Hollywood Boulevard and Cosmo Street. For many years, until the 1920s skyscrapers were built, it was the largest building in Hollywood and was headquarters to the American Society of Cinematographers.

W. F. Markham, manufacturer and promoter of the CHALLENGER; in 1886, the first commercially successful B.B gun.

He invested heavily in real estate and, by his death in 1930, owned over one hundred parcels of land, all leased for ninety-nine years. It is likely that those leases were held by companies in the film industry. In 1927 he built a mansion, Homeland, on a seven-acre lot at 1405 E. Mountain St. in Glendale at a cost of $50,000. The 7,500 square foot gated home, with an exterior of glazed brick, featured seven bedrooms, nine bathrooms, a six-car garage and a 1,100 square foot guest apartment.

During the Great Depression, sales at both Daisy and King dropped thirty percent. Cass Hough proposed that Daisy acquire King Manufacturing and market the King line through direct retail sales, mail order and premium businesses. With the sale complete in 1931, only a few key pieces of equipment were moved across the railroad tracks to Daisy. Daisy continued to produce a line of King air rifles up until World War II and used the old Markham plant for storage and shipping.

That's our story and we're sticking to it.
How boring Daisy corporate history would be without these colorful stories. The fact is that no history of Daisy would be complete without including the early years of the Plymouth Iron Windmill Company and the Markham Company. Because the first Markham gun was produced in 1886 and because Daisy executives and later Daisy acquired Markham (by then doing business as King Manufacturing) Daisy traces its BB gun history to that 1886 date.

Yes, the truth, as best it's known, is that the Daisy brand and product are named due to a colloquial saying of the 1880s, "Boy, that's a Daisy." And, yes, due to the acquisition of King, Daisy has been in the airgun business since 1886.

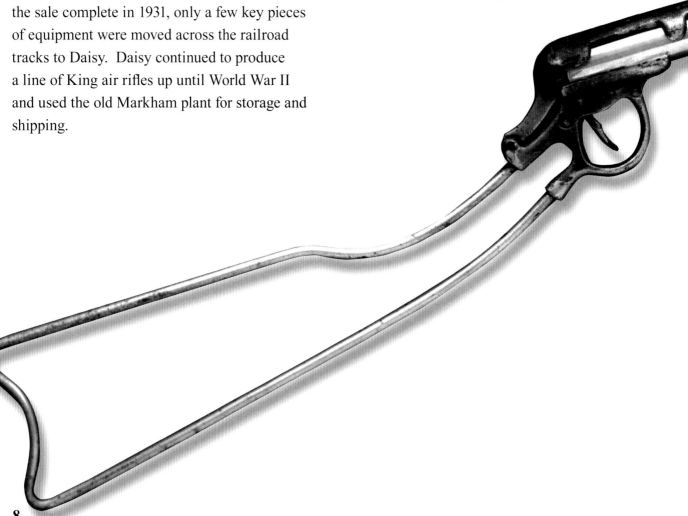

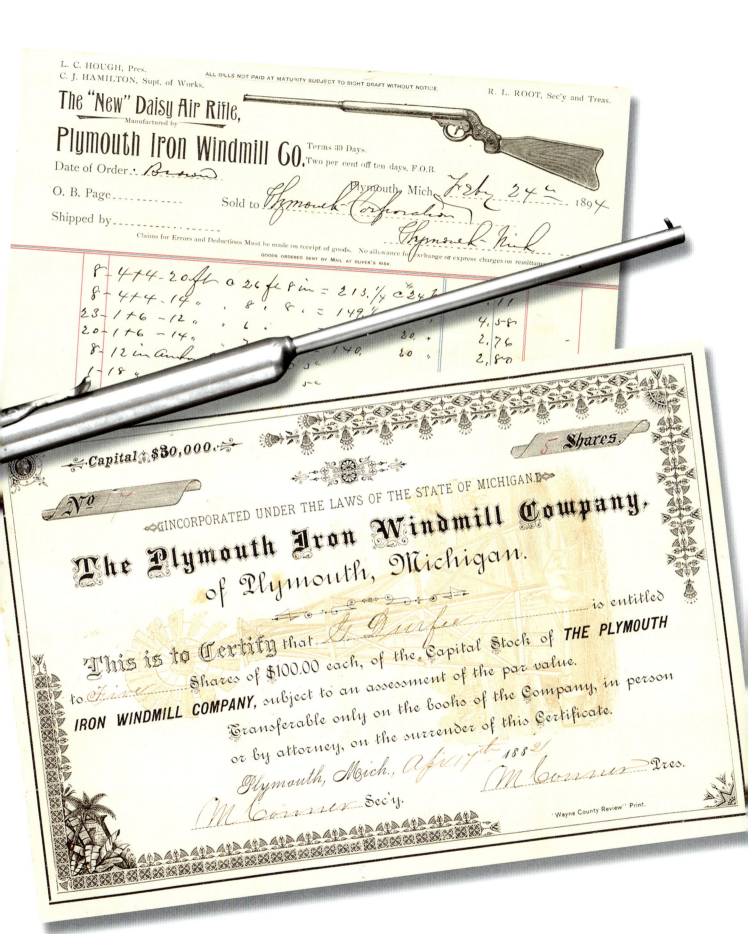

Chapter 2
Historical Significance

Putting Things into Perspective
It would be over four years after the Plymouth Iron Windmill Company was founded that the statue "Liberty Enlightening the World" (the Statue of Liberty) was dedicated in New York harbor on October 28, 1886. That same year, the Markham Air Rifle Company was established along the Pere Marquette Railroad tracks in Plymouth, Michigan.

Daisy, as a company and as a product, has endured the test of time, seen the passage of many significant and historical events and been party to more than a few of them.

Called to Serve
Throughout American history, Daisy has had its share of U.S. Government contracts for production. With the surprise attack on Pearl Harbor by the Imperial Japanese Navy on the morning of December 7, 1941, the United States was drawn into World War II. Within days, regulations were issued to American manufacturers, prohibiting the use of strategic materials, such as steel, for the production of non-essential products. When the existing inventory of parts and raw steel at Daisy was exhausted, further production and commercial sale of BBs and BB guns was prohibited.

In a display case in the Daisy Museum today is one sample of nearly every part Daisy manufactured directly for the War Department and as a sub-contractor for other manufacturers.

The company made gaskets and dies for AC Spark Plug Division, parts for electrical switches for Square D Manufacturing Company, precision ball races for Palmer-Bee Company, washers for Ligon Brothers and dies for Bendix Aviation, Nippert Electric Company and Pilgrim Drawn Steel Corporation. Additionally, Daisy produced two billion, three hundred million BBs which were used by the Army and Navy Air Forces in flexible gunnery simulators. BB training machine guns (not made by Daisy) were used to train aerial gunners. Powered by compressed air from a tank, they fired BBs at a rate of five hundred per minute.

An honor roll plaque, on display in the Daisy Museum, once hung in the lobby of the company's offices. It honors, by name, those who served their country in the armed forces during World War II. The honor roll includes Colonel Cass S. Hough, grandson of the company's founder, who was stationed in England with the 8th Air Force. Rest assured those who remained employed at Daisy during the war years also did their part to support the war effort by manufacturing the tools our servicemen took into battle.

11

Ball Bearing Contract

As our nation became involved in the Vietnam War, there was considerable need for anti-personnel bomblets which were machine-filled with ground ball bearings. The bomblets were dropped from airplanes and primarily targeted anti-aircraft positions. Some were designed to explode at a pre-determined, low altitude. Another type would fall to the ground then explode within minutes, a technique used to keep the enemy from entering an area. The ball bearing precision, consistent within one ten-thousandths of an inch (0.0001), was necessary in order to accommodate the bomb filling technique.

Manufacturers were scrambling to meet demand for the ball bearings; however, the lead time to purchase a header was eighteen months. Daisy had its own patterns and could have castings made, machine them and have new headers online in about six months, giving the company the ability to get into production a year before others could.

Daisy was contacted by Wright Patterson Air Force Base in Dayton, Ohio, regarding becoming a supplier of ball bearings for these anti-personnel bombs. Dick Daniel flew to Dayton to visit with ten colonels and present Daisy's capabilities to the Air Force. The Air Force was willing to make a one million dollar investment in a separate, free-standing 12,000 square foot facility in order for the company to have the capacity to meet their demand for ball bearings. Daisy turned down the offer, believing that an expansion of the current facility would be more cost-efficient and provide better quality control.

At the same time Dick was in Dayton, Murchison Brothers, parent company of Daisy, was being acquired by Victor Comptometer. Federal

Trade Commission rules precluded Dick from disclosing the potential sale. He was in no position to commit to production or to sign a contract.

Daisy's President, Cass Hough, was on vacation in the Bahamas and Dick and Frank Tarr arranged to meet with him there. Cass spoke with both the Victor Comptometer and the Murchison boards of directors because the necessary plant expansion and the proposed U.S. Air Force contract would have material impact on the company's sale. With approval of both boards, Dick contacted Wright Patterson from the Bahamas and finalized the terms of the contract.

Daisy proceeded with a plant expansion, upgraded electrical facilities and was able to add over thirty headers, with priority assistance from the U.S. Government to secure the grinders. Five months later, with the facility expanded and upgraded and all of the headers in place, Daisy began producing to meet demand, yet did not receive a contract until the day before the first delivery of ball bearings.

Sixty thousand pounds of wire were processed into ball bearings each day. Steel from Kansas City arrived by rail car; one car every two days. Daisy was the nation's low cost producer for ball bearings. During the four years in which Daisy produced ball bearings for Wright Patterson, the company lost the bid for the contract more than once.

However, because other companies failed to meet demand, Daisy continuously shipped the product over the four year period. The first contract for $2,647,500, awarded on March 30, 1967, was the largest single order Daisy had ever received. Over the course of four years, the company would produce thirty-five million balls valued at eleven million dollars.

Instinctive Shooting

Another way in which Daisy supported the armed forces during the Vietnam Era was by supplying sightless Model 99 BB guns for the Quick Kill training program.

U. S. TROOPS TRAIN WITH DAISY B.B GUNS -- Typical of the U. S. Army Training Program now installed at all basic training centers in this country is this line of GIs training with modified Daisy B.B guns. The program, conceived by the Continental Army Command in cooperation with Daisy, is the preliminary step in teaching troops to become marksmen. Similar training programs are being conducted in Vietnam and other allied countries. The Daisy guns cost one-tenth the price of the M-16s, and 475 B.Bs can be fired for the cost of one round of live ammunition. (Please credit official U.S. Army photo.)

--30--

5-15-68

NEWS RELEASE
DAISY/HEDDON
ROGERS, ARKANSAS 72756
DIVISION VICTOR COMPTOMETER CORPORATION

VICTOR 50TH YEAR-1968

FOR FURTHER INFORMATION CONTACT:
John R. Powers, Jr. Vice President
AC 501-636-1200 --- TWX 910-720-7993

Mike Jennings initially presented the instinctive shooting program to the Armed Forces at Fort Benning, Georgia. Shortly thereafter, training centers all over the country were placing orders for sightless Daisy Model 99 BB guns and BBs. Most recruits for the Vietnam War recall learning how to shoot instinctively, not with an M-16 but with a Daisy.

The training regimen was, and still is, a highly effective one. By removing the sights from a BB gun, concentrating not on the gun but on the target, and repeatedly cocking, consistently mounting and firing the gun – without taking ones eyes off of the target – anyone can learn to shoot instinctively.

Where Were You When…?
There are a number of significant events in American history that prompt each of us to recall where we were and what we were doing. Certainly 9/11, as the date September 11, 2001, has come to be known, is one of those events.

Like so many Americans, Daisy employees were just arriving at work when radio news reports were beginning to erroneously report that a small private plane had apparently veered off course and struck one of the twin towers of the World Trade Center in Manhattan. Within minutes, all of America would know that our country was under a terrorist attack.

Ray Hobbs had been at the helm of Daisy for just over two months. He encouraged the Daisy staff to assemble in the company's conference room in order to have access to the latest television coverage. For the time being, business travel was cancelled.

Within hours, President George Bush had made a passionate nationwide plea for Americans to respond to the needs of the families directly impacted by this tragedy. He specifically mentioned a new 9/11 Fund, established through the United Way in Manhattan. Ray Hobbs made it clear that, as an old American company, Daisy should respond and asked that a plan of action be put in place.

Several weeks prior, Daisy's supplier, which had been retained to apply camouflage pattern film to the Model 840 Grizzly BB guns, had covered one Model 840 with a montage of American flags and sent it to the company for consideration. At the time, the company didn't see a market for the

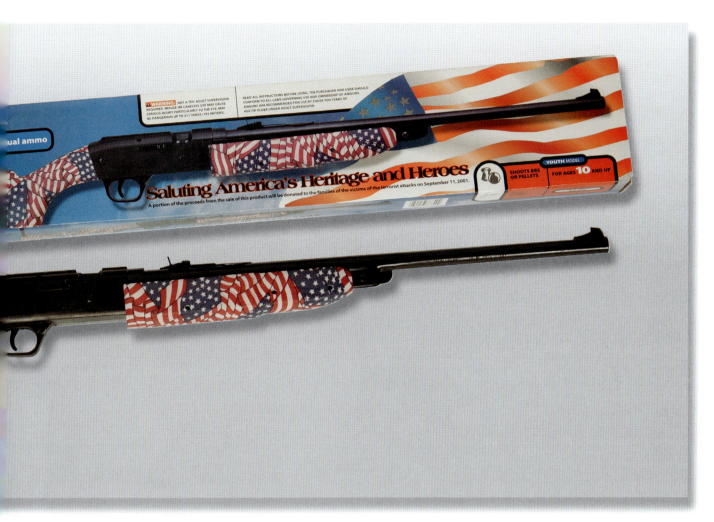

gun. On 9/11, within hours, that prototype gun had a name, a beautiful package and a purpose. It became Daisy's response to this significant tragedy.

Immediately, orders were placed for the flag patterned stocks and forearms, necessary to assemble 1,350 of the guns. The package design for the "American Spirit" was completed within twenty-four hours. It featured an American flag and, of course, a photo of the gun. A statement on the package made it clear that this gun represented Daisy's response to the 9/11 attacks: "A portion of the proceeds from the sale of this product will be donated to the families of the victims of the terrorist attacks on September 11, 2001." Daisy calculated the potential proceeds and mailed the check within twenty-four hours to the 9/11 Fund.

The Daisy American Spirit was never sold through retail stores. Shortly after 9/11, the company began receiving an onslaught of requests from fire and police departments seeking donations for fundraising events related to the 9/11 tragedy. The American Spirit was the perfect response for Daisy and, no doubt, was instrumental in helping to raise hundreds of thousands of dollars. When only a few hundred of the guns remained, they were donated to the Rogers Daisy Airgun Museum so that collectors could own a small piece of Daisy history and American history.

Homeland Security Comes to Rogers

Following the September 11, 2001, attack on the twin towers and Pentagon came the threat of bioterrorism attacks. Letters containing anthrax spores were received by political and media targets beginning September 18 and throughout October. The bioterrorism attacks were responsible for nineteen people being infected and for the deaths of five, including two postal workers. Daisy's President and C.E.O. Ray Hobbs had been in Washington, D.C., in the Senate Building during this period of time when the building was evacuated for suspected anthrax. He returned home under instruction to see his physician and begin a course of the antibiotic Cipro.

The Federal Bureau of Investigation launched its Amerithrax investigation and cautioned American companies to be suspicious of letters or packages which were not addressed to any particular person. At Daisy, mail with an incomplete address, not addressed to a specific name or from unidentified senders, would be placed in a plastic tub with a lid and held for inspection by, or return to, the post office.

On Friday morning, May 19, 2006, a letter with a handwritten address was received by Daisy. The postage stamps and the typed letter appeared to be foreign, possibly Turkish, and there was a website, ending in the suffix ".ru" at the bottom of the letter. That, in and of itself, did not arouse suspicion as the company did business in Turkey and many other foreign countries. Daisy's receptionist opened the envelope only to have white powder fall out on her desk. Suspecting the worst, she followed company policy by alerting the company's safety committee including the human resources department and chief operating officer.

The local police and fire departments were called and immediately responded with a hazardous materials team. All employees were evacuated from the building into the parking lot where they were detained for observation. Those employees were instructed to call anyone who had been in the building that morning and ask them to return for observation. The front door to the building was taped off by Homeland Security personnel, and employees were not allowed to re-enter, even to retrieve their keys, purses or cell phones. They were moved into the warehouse area adjacent to the offices where they remained until dismissed late that afternoon.

Meanwhile, a hazardous materials crew bagged the suspicious letter then thoroughly inspected the lobby and the entire building with testing equipment. Four employees, who may have had contact with the white powder, were kept inside the building in a room adjacent to the lobby where their blood pressure and heart rate were monitored. The police officer who first responded to the scene was quarantined with them. They were periodically questioned regarding potential side effects.

Using plastic film, the hazardous materials crew constructed a shower room in the parking lot with a tunnel connected to the front doorway.

One at a time, the four employees and one police officer walked out to the shower enclosure, removed their clothing, stood in a plastic pool and showered, using a hand-held showerhead and water from a fire truck. They were then provided a towel and gown and transported by ambulance to St. Mary's Hospital in Rogers, where they once again showered.

The group remained together at the hospital, on monitors and under observation until about 4:00 p.m. At that time, with the powder having been determined to most likely be pulverized laundry detergent, they were released. Daisy's offices remained under the control of Homeland Security and it would be Monday afternoon before the company would have access to the building. Daisy never learned by whom the letter was sent or why the company was targeted for this hoax.

Drill Rifles

In 2001 Daisy secured a contract with the U.S. Navy to produce a nearly indestructible drill rifle to be utilized by the U.S. Navy JROTC honor guards, color guards and drill teams nationwide.

Within a matter of years, Daisy had secured similar contracts with the Army, Marines and Air Force. At first glance the Daisy drill rifle looks like a fully functional 1903-A3 Springfield rifle with a black synthetic stock. However, the only functional moving part is the bolt. The barrel itself is a solid rod. The design and durable steel components and synthetic stock make this drill rifle capable of withstanding the abuse that is inherent in drill team use. In fact, the prescribed durability test includes dropping the drill rifle onto a concrete surface twenty-five times from a height of twelve feet, at a forty-five degree angle, onto its butt and muzzle. Additionally, it must pass a six foot drop test, at a ninety degree angle, onto its butt and muzzle. The guns must meet or exceed these endurance tests, without significant separation, cracking, bending, warping, denting, splintering, chipping or breakage and remain able to perform their intended use.

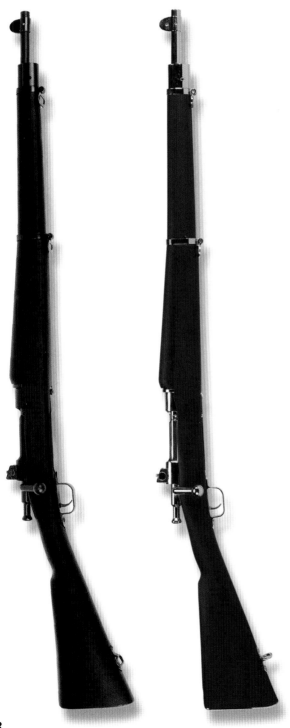

Slingshots in Iraq

Following the September 11, 2001, terrorist attacks, the United States believed that Iraq may have been linked to the Al-Qaeda terrorist network. The U.S. was also convinced that Saddam Hussein was harboring chemical and biological weapons of mass destruction and developing nuclear weapons. When Iraq failed to respond to President Bush's demand to prove that they were disarming weapons, U.S. and British forces, as a part of a coalition effort, attacked Baghdad in March 2003.

In November 2003 Daisy received an email from a young U.S. soldier stationed in Iraq. This Specialist, a contract supply officer, was from Oklahoma City, was a fan of Daisy products and requested that the company send him some product catalogs for members of his company to review. Of course the company complied and sent not only Daisy catalogs but lots of hunting and gun magazines. Once the catalogs arrived, the soldier requested a quantity of Daisy slingshots. Camped on the outskirts of Baghdad, the slingshots were used for recreation, to control wild dogs coming into their camp and to retaliate against insurgents armed with rocks and bottles. Daisy sent enough slingshots, ammunition and targets for the entire unit to use.

Believing the company had discovered a niche market for slingshots, Daisy contacted the Marine Corps Weapons Development Division at Quantico, Virginia, the lead agency with a sub-agency for testing and development of non-lethal weapons such as Tasers, Phasers, net guns, batons and bean bag guns used for non-lethal personnel control.

While the Weapons Development Division had no problem with supply officers ordering slingshots, they were not interested in issuing them as secondary non-lethal weapons. Rather, they were focused on the development of non-lethal munitions to be used in primary weapons. The M-16, for example, had an M203 chamber into which various non-lethal munitions could be loaded. Those on patrol in Baghdad typically loaded both lethal and non-lethal loads. Non-lethal loads included rubber bullets and sting loads. The Weapons Development Division was not looking for additional delivery systems because they didn't want to burden soldiers with extra gear.

While Daisy slingshots were never standard issue, the company is proud that, for at least one company stationed on the outskirts of Baghdad, its products provided both recreation and a degree of protection.

Daisy's history is, in fact, securely woven into the fabric of America's heritage. The company is grateful for each opportunity it has had to serve its nation with expertise and product.

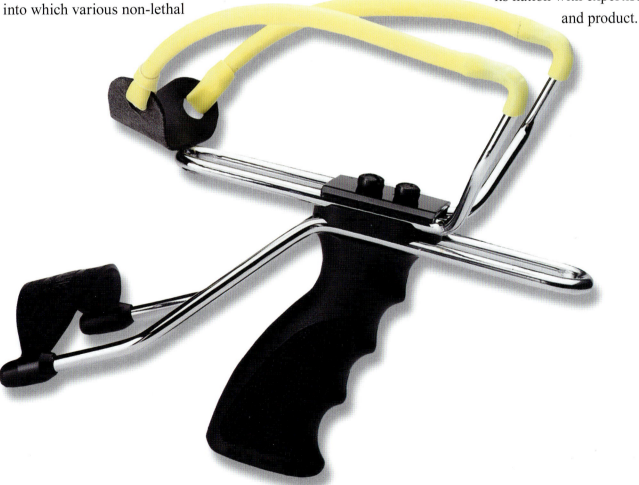

Chapter 3

What's in the Box?

Working for Daisy is an honor. The name recognition is incredible. Daisy staff that travel on company business have to make a conscious decision whether or not to travel in a shirt with a Daisy logo on it. If they do, it's likely the person next to them on the plane will have a Daisy story or two to tell. Daisy staff members never tire of hearing the line, "My first gun was a Daisy!" Once a Daisy employee anxiously pointed out to the flight attendant that it was the pilot, not the employee, who brought up the subject of shooting Daisy BB guns while standing outside the cockpit of a commercial airplane.

The company values the Daisy brand and guards it with their best efforts, striving for dominance, visibility and consistency of the logo. However, while Daisy can control the consistent appearance of its logo, the brand itself is much larger. Its perception is, somewhat, beyond the company's complete control.

What's in a Name

The brand is not just the word Daisy, with a red bullseye in the center of the letter D. That's the Daisy logo. Rather, the brand is the culmination of what consumers believe and feel about the company and the product and the emotional tie they have with it. When they see a Daisy logo, an ad, a package on the shelf or an online review of a new product, their perceptions

are based not only on the information they encounter at that time but on the grand total of their own past experiences.

The founder of a famous pizza delivery business once addressed his management team, stating, "We're in the <u>delivery</u> business. We just happen to take pizzas with us." In making that statement, he took the emphasis off of the ingredients (very common tangible commodities) and put the emphasis on what the customer perceived and valued: a timely delivery experience. Today, their brand is synonymous with timely delivery.

In a way, Daisy is like that company. They make a good pizza and Daisy makes a good airgun. But what the company really delivers inside the BB gun package is an experience which most people will never forget. It might be the first shot they took or a memorable moment with a parent or grandparent who has now passed on to larger life. They might recall a mentor or a coach who taught them a whole lot more than how to punch a hole in a paper target.

Life Lessons Learned
There are important life-changing lessons to be learned with a Daisy BB gun. Shooting teaches patience, which is an attribute that will help young people with a difficult job assignment or unreasonable boss someday. They learn self-control, which will help them be a better friend, spouse or parent. They are taught responsibility, which will gain them the respect of others. And, shooting requires discipline, which will mold their character and help them stand-out from the crowd. The results: better students, better relationships, better employees and true

successes – on the range and in the things that really matter in life.

Daisy knows that it works. The company has been introduced to numerous adults who - ten, twenty and thirty years ago - were on a five meter shooting team. Today, they have confessed, they can attribute their rise through ranks of the military, their success in business, their ability to work with and manage other people and their rewarding relationships with friends and family to the character traits which they developed while on a Daisy five meter BB gun team.

Sure, Daisy makes a great BB gun. But the business the company is really in is perpetuating a great sport, changing lives, teaching life lessons and building character traits that will last a lifetime. That's a lot to pack into a BB gun box, but it's all part of the perception of what a Daisy is and what the company stands for. That's what makes the logo so readily-recognized and the brand so loved.

The Keys to a Successful Brand

So, what does it take to not just sustain a business for 125 years but to build a Daisy brand that is known by and loved by generations of users? The consecutive years in business alone are an admirable measure of success and a source of great pride. However, just a few minutes of internet research will inform you that while Daisy and other household brands you might easily call to mind are old, they don't hold the record. In fact, the oldest recorded U.S. business is the Avedis Zildjian Cymbal Company of Norwell, Massachusetts, started in 1623. So why is Daisy a household word and Zildjian not?

In the mid 2000s Trophy Research, Inc. was retained to assess the impact, value and effectiveness of the Daisy brand. They surveyed a pure panel of outdoor enthusiasts, both geographically and demographically diverse. Following the tabulation of results, Trophy Research proclaimed that Daisy was a superbrand. They defined a superbrand as one which garners in excess of 75% unaided awareness within its product category. (Unaided awareness is tested by asking interviewees to name an airgun company, without listing any options.)

Becoming a Superbrand

In the Trophy Research findings, Daisy's unaided top-of-mind awareness average was calculated to be 82.30%. Daisy's closest competitor earned an average unaided top-of-mind awareness of 9.72%! As a superbrand, Daisy is in the company of recognizable corporate giants. A superbrand is one that is always in the purchase consideration set when a purchase is to be made within its product category.

There are several factors which contribute to establishing and maintaining superbrand status. Being the first to launch a product in a category (a category that later becomes widely accepted) is, in most cases, the first criteria for becoming a superbrand. People remember firsts … the first president, the first man on the moon –both are easy to recall, but naming the second for either is a bigger challenge for most. The same is true for brands within a category. The first name people know/associate with a particular category of goods is often times the one they remember.

With its start in the late 1800s, Daisy was among the first to enter the airgun market and the first to widely establish a brand.

Being the most prominent marketer in the category for decades also helps to ensure a brand's recognition and acceptance. Early efforts at branding and innovative marketing strategies included advertising in prominent youth magazines and comic books as

When a brand has a strong history/heritage, the likelihood is increased that the preference for the brand will be passed down from one generation to the next. Daisy takes great pride in the fact that, from generation to generation, a Daisy BB gun has been the first gun for most Americans.

From Generation to Generation

The Daisy brand has endured for generations because it exudes tradition as well as quality and value. It has endured because the brand doesn't just stand for a group of products. Rather, the brand stands for the experiences and the memories associated with the use of the product. A Daisy BB gun is, by design, meant to be used under the supervision of a mentor. Generations of Daisy shooters value the memories they have of learning to shoot, shoulder to shoulder, with a parent or grandparent. Today's most successful hunters and most accomplished marksmen will tell you they took their first shot with a Daisy. Even members of the USA Shooting team who represent our country at international shooting well as many successful licensed product promotions featuring famous western and Hollywood personalities. Certainly the creation of a Daisy Red Ryder BB gun created synergy with the comic strip, comic book and big screen success enjoyed by the famous Red Ryder character.

sports competitions will tell you they got their start with a Daisy Red Ryder or Model 25.

Most of them will tell you they were mentored by an adult who was an important figure in their life. Learning to shoot is an experience of a lifetime that builds a unique bond between parent and child, between grandparent and child or between mentor and child. Let's face it: shooting is fun. There's something about plinking in the backyard that brings a smile to the face of every child and adult.

People typically like a particular brand because it's what they had and what they trusted when they were growing up. Grandparents and parents are, therefore, likely to want their children to own a Daisy because it's the brand they had growing up. The generational aspect of the Daisy brand has been further strengthened with the launch of the movie *A Christmas Story*, and is reinforced every year as this movie receives countless airings leading up to the Christmas season.

A Daisy BB gun is one of the most memorable gifts a youngster will ever receive for a birthday or Christmas. While you may not be able to remember what you got for Christmas as a child each year, chances are good that you remember, like Ralphie Parker, the day you found your Daisy under the Christmas tree. Often referred to as "America's favorite Christmas gift," what makes a Daisy so memorable is that receiving it is a rite of passage. Getting your first Daisy meant that your parents acknowledged that you were ready for the responsibility of an airgun.

Consistent Branding Counts

Maintaining superbrand status is an ongoing challenge, and maintaining quality is critical to that effort. Brands are built over decades, not years. Smart brand marketers continue to support and build their brand both with a steady stream of relevant, quality new products and through high-quality brand marketing. Research on the Daisy brand over consecutive years had established that more consumers were aware of the brand each year.

It was based on this research that Daisy developed the slogan, "Take Pride. It's a Daisy." Early research had proven that the generational aspect of the Daisy brand was significant. Most outdoor enthusiasts grew up with a Daisy brand BB gun, which was either passed down to them or was purchased for them because their parent or grandparent owned one. Research indicated a significant pride associated with having one's children enjoy the same brand of BB gun they enjoyed as a youngster.

What Does Daisy Mean to You?

What's in the Daisy box nestled behind the tree on Christmas morning? What life experiences race through your mind when you stand in a sporting goods store and scan the Daisy packages? History, nostalgia, family memories, team experiences, some serious life lessons and a lot of fun are all part of our brand. **That's what's in the Daisy box.**

Chapter 4
BBs and Ball Bearings

Probably the most common misperception about BBs is that the two Bs stand for ball bearing. True, a ball bearing is typically made of steel and is round but, of course, ball bearings come in a myriad of sizes. BB is actually a specific size of shot, originally 0.180 (eighteen one hundredths of an inch in diameter) lead shotgun shot.

When W.F. Markham made his first BB gun in 1886 – the one to which Daisy traces its involvement in the BB gun business – he simply chose a readily available size of shot: size BB. And when Clarence Hamilton tried to improve on the Markham wooden gun design with his own "Challenger" model, he utilized the same size shot. Even when he took his wire frame top-cocker, destined to become the first "Daisy" model, into Lewis Cass Hough's office at The Plymouth Iron Windmill Company, he dropped a size BB lead shot into the muzzle end of the slightly tapered barrel. For years, Daisy refrained from referring to their guns as BB guns because the company thought the phrase to be demeaning.

Around the turn of the century, Daisy began ordering special lead shot, averaging .175 in diameter. The smaller sized, lighter weight shot improved velocities significantly. Until this time, most BB gun ammunition was sold in bulk in hardware stores.

Ball Bearings Damage Guns
Other than the fact that the words ball and bearing start with the letter B, there is one other reason this legend may have been perpetuated. Early in his career, Cass Hough worked in the inspection department, a department which, today, the company refers to as the recovery department. From Cass's description, it doesn't sound like much has changed

in the nature of BB gun returns. Even though the company suspected that a gun had been abused, they made the repair and returned the gun to its owner. However, Cass began to detect a pattern of common abuse, resulting in shot tubes being split open. He suspected that the shooter had used an oversize steel ball bearing instead of lead BB shot. Finding steel ball bearings stuck in the shot tube confirmed his suspicions.

Hough logged the returns and determined that the majority of these guns were coming from the Minneapolis area, home to a ball bearing manufacturer, the American Ball Company. A trip to Minneapolis confirmed suspicions that boys were recovering rejected ball bearings from a scrap heap behind the American Ball facility.

Bulls Eye BBs

Shortly thereafter, American Ball marketed the "Bulls Eye" brand of BBs with 0.171 to 0.173-inch (4.4 mm) diameters.

Photo courtesy of Bob Boccaccio

The lighter weight made them superior to comparable lead BB shot, and the lower cost contributed to their success at retail. However, lack of quality control resulted in inconsistently sized BBs and, once again, product returns to Daisy increased. To rectify the situation, Daisy became the sole agent for American Ball, receiving a commission on sales and a portion of the profit. Finally, in 1939 Daisy acquired the assets of American Ball and moved the shot operation to Plymouth.

Changing from lead shot to steel BBs created new challenges for Daisy. The swaged shot seat that gripped lead shot in the breech was not effective at holding steel BBs. A wire spring and later a magnet were used to retain the BB until it was fired.

How BBs Are Made
A BB actually begins as a roll of steel wire. The wire is fed into a header, where it is initially cut into length by knives. These slugs are then headed, compressing the short piece of wire from both ends with enough force to turn the wire slug into a sphere. The heading procedure often leaves dimples at opposite sides of the BB at what used to be the ends of the chopped wire. Edging sometimes remains around the circumference. The headed shot drops into a collection pan and is dumped into hoppers. The shot is poured from the hoppers into the flasher. In the flasher, grooved grinding wheels round the shot and remove skirts and nipples. The shot is passed through the flasher several times. Adjusting the pressure of the grinding wheels controls the shot size. Bricks of zinc are loaded into the electroplating bath where BBs are introduced for plating. Final screening ensures that each BB still conforms to specifications. BBs are rinsed and dried under lights before being sent to the shot pack department.

Some of the earliest BBs made by Daisy in 1933 – 1934 were copper plated in order to prevent the steel balls from rusting and marketed under the brand Copprotect. In 1964 Daisy BBs were marketed in a bright silver tube under the Lube Plated name. In mid-1965 Daisy began marketing Golden Bullseye BBs, which were zinc plated with an orange dye added to achieve the gold color. In 1985 the dye was eliminated and Daisy BBs became known as Quick Silver BBs. Today's Daisy BBs remain silver in color and have been marketed under the brand names Daisy MaxSpeed and Daisy PrecisionMax.

Improving BBs

Probably the most significant force in driving improvement in BB quality was Daisy's improvement in the accuracy of the BB gun. When Daisy introduced the Model 99 (today, the Model 499 AVANTI Champion) as a five meter match competition BB gun, young shooters and coaches began demanding a higher quality, more accurate BB. Daisy responded with the No. 515 Precision Ground Shot, though distribution was initially restricted to clubs and competitors.

During the Vietnam War, the company's capacity for production of BBs of ball bearing quality was increased to meet demand of an Air Force contract. Shortly after that contract ended, Daisy's capacity was absorbed by demand for steel shot from the firearms industry. Daisy remained the lowest cost steel ball producer in the United States and, consequently, produced steel shot in several sizes for most of the major manufacturers of shotgun shells.

Moving to Salem, Missouri

When the Daisy plant on South Eighth Street in Rogers, Arkansas, was sold in 1999, the BB production remained at that facility. Daisy's assembly operation was, at that time, relocated in Neosho, Missouri. In 2003, under an agreement to vacate the former Daisy plant on Eighth Street and in an effort to improve quality and efficiency, Daisy relocated its BB production to Salem, Missouri. In Salem, the production facility was near a plater and closer to the Neosho, Missouri, shipping facility. On March 26, 2003, Salem, Missouri, mayor, Gary Brown, and Daisy President & C.E.O., Ray Hobbs shot the ribbon to ceremonially announce the opening of Daisy's Salem BB Production Facility.

During this same time period, however, China began major infrastructure improvements and monopolized the purchase of U.S. steel, subsidizing its cost to Chinese industry. Essentially China was selling steel to its industrial processors more inexpensively than a U.S. company could buy the same U.S. steel domestically. Daisy constantly monitored and compared the cost of steel wire available in the United States with the cost of finished BBs manufactured in China. For three years Daisy struggled and suffered losses just in order to compete with a domestically produced BB.

The closing of the Salem, Missouri, BB Production Facility on January 31, 2006, was a direct result of a one hundred percent increase in the cost of domestic steel which the company had endured for over two years. Competition in the marketplace had forced Daisy to maintain their price on BBs and prevented the company from passing along this drastic increase in steel cost to its retail customers. Daisy began importing a percentage of BB ammunition in order to reduce the average cost. Even so, the company continued to suffer the impact of profit loss for almost two years in order to preserve jobs at the Salem facility for as long as possible.

Addressing the employees and community leaders, Ray Hobbs stated, "Regrettably, high steel prices and market factors outside of our control have forced us to take this action. We have very much enjoyed working in the Salem community. I don't have anything but positive comments regarding our experiences working with the Mayor, City Aldermen, the Salem Chamber of Commerce, the Economic Development and the Industrial Development Authority, Dent County Work Force Development, Dent County Commissioners and the Regional Planning Commission. And, we've been fortunate to have worked with a team of dedicated, hard working employees. I'm confident that we made every effort, studied every possible option and delayed this action just as long as possible."

BBs Today

In 2006 the BB packaging operation was integrated into the assembly facility in Neosho, Missouri, and moved to Rogers, Arkansas, in 2007 when the assembly facility was relocated.

Amazingly, the same machinery acquired from The American Ball Company in Minneapolis was relocated to the Plymouth, Michigan, Daisy plant in 1939 and moved to Rogers, Arkansas, in 1958. That machinery, carefully maintained, was still in operation at the Daisy plant on Eighth Street through 2002 and moved to Salem, Missouri, in 2003.

Over the years, Daisy had as many as one hundred and ten headers. The maintenance programs called for ten headers to be pulled each year, approximately one per month. The header would be taken out of service, disassembled,

rebuilt and put back into service. Each header had the capability of making two hundred and fifty BBs per minute. At the peak of BB production, fifty-five million BBs were produced each day.

Today, bulk finished BBs are imported from China in fifty-five gallon drums, weighing 2,000 lbs. and holding approximately 2,600,000 BBs. BBs are screened to cull any mis-sized BBs or BBs with imperfections before they are packaged. One automated packaging line fills, caps and tapes the iconic 350-count BB tube. A second automated packaging line fills plastic bottles, then caps, labels and shrink wraps them before they are case packed for shipment.

While plastic boxes, chipboard boxes, milk cartons and plastic bottles have all been used successfully to market BBs in much larger, more cost-effective quantities, it is the cardboard tube which remains the most universally recognized BB package.

Chapter 5
Ralphie Got it Wrong

© 1983 Metro-Goldwyn-Mayer, United Artists Entertainment Company

For the past several years, the movie *A Christmas Story* has aired twenty-four hours a day on television on Christmas Eve day. Often Daisy is asked if the movie has any effect on sales. While it certainly can't hurt and while the company would prefer it to air over the Thanksgiving weekend instead, there is no doubt that a Daisy Red Ryder is a top selling Christmas gift, year after year, with or without a movie airing.

What's significant about the movie is that the gun for which Ralphie so ardently lobbies never existed.

In 1983 MGM produced the movie based on material taken from Jean Shepherd's humorous short stories "In God We Trust, All Others Pay Cash" and "Wanda Hickey's Night of Golden Memories" as well as some unpublished stories from

TOP: Buck Jones model.
BOTTOM: One of three Daisy Red Ryder movie prop guns.

his WOR radio talk show. The title of the movie, set in the early 1940s, became *A Christmas Story*. In the movie, the main character, a young boy named Ralphie Parker, asked Santa Claus and his parents for *"an official Red Ryder carbine-action 200-shot range model air rifle with a compass in the stock, and this thing which tells time."*

While the story is not autobiographical, Shepherd did base his stories on personal recollections of growing up in the Midwest. The only problem was the Daisy Red Ryder never had a compass or sundial in the stock. The gun which had those distinctive features was the Buck Jones, which was a pump gun, not a lever action gun like the Red Ryder.

Reality Imitating Art
Failing to convince the production company that the script should be changed, Daisy agreed to inset a compass in the stock, silkscreen a sundial on the stock and add a copper forearm band and a copper front sight band to three guns to be used as props in the movie. Orin Ribar, customer service manager, had some of the old Model 1938 Red Ryders (made from 1972 to 1978) which looked very similar to the old No. 111, Model 40 Red Ryders. He had the stock from an old Buck Jones gun photographed in order to create a silkscreen pattern. Daisy staff routed the stock, inserted the compass and silk-screened the sundial onto the Red Ryder.

Once this prototype was created, John Ford coordinated the production of the three movie prop guns. In fact, he recalls that his wife Sara painted the forearm bands and front sight bands for these three guns to make them look more like the old models. One of the movie's three prop guns remains in the Daisy Museum. Based on the immediate popularity of the movie, Daisy committed to produce the Red Ryder with a compass and sundial in the stock for the balance of 1983 and all of 1984.

Movie Mementos
In 2003 and 2008, on the occasions of the twentieth and twenty-fifth anniversaries of this gun, the Daisy Museum produced a limited number of Daisy Red Ryders, just like the ones Daisy made in 1983 and 1984, specially engraved with the anniversary years. These guns were marketed exclusively to collectors.

In 2003 Warner Home Video sent a California film crew to Rogers, Arkansas, to tour the assembly facility and Daisy Museum and interview Daisy retirees John Ford and Orin Ribar as well as Daisy employees Steven Ribar and Susan Gardner Johnston about their experiences working for Daisy. The resulting 20th Anniversary Special Edition two DVD set included the movie plus a documentary with cast member commentaries, Daisy Family interviews, interactive trivia and the original theatrical trailer.

The Daisy Museum is fortunate to have several artifacts from the movie's production - including a poster, concession stand card, black and white photography taken on the set during production of the movie and a photo showing Daisy employees attending a premier showing of the movie in Rogers, Arkansas.

Are You Ready for Christmas?
There's a little bit of Ralphie in each of us, remembering how we aggressively lobbied our parents for our first Daisy and not having been certain of our success until the last package was opened one Christmas morning.

Chapter 6
The Daisy Family

If you've ever worked for Daisy, you probably just turned to this chapter to see if your name is mentioned. In the city of Rogers, Arkansas, just about everyone has had a relative work for Daisy. Listing the names of all of the thousands of people who had a hand in the success of Daisy would require a book of its own.

Typically, when a person identifies himself or herself as having worked at Daisy they will talk about who was president of the company when they were there and they will refer to their co-workers as their Daisy Family.

> **"** ...they will refer to their co-workers as their "Daisy Family".

Strong Leadership

Daisy has been fortunate to have, as members of its Family, some very intelligent people, some ingenious, inventive, innovative people, some creative people, some dedicated and many hard working people. And, the company has been fortunate to have had a handful of tremendously insightful and dynamic leaders. Surprisingly, but perhaps a contributing factor to its success, Daisy Manufacturing Company has had only ten presidents:

M. Conner, President, Plymouth Iron Windmill Company	1882 – 1883
O.A. Fraser	1884 – 1885
C.B. Crosby	1886
H.W. Baker	1887 – 1888
M. Conner	1889 – 1892
L.C. Hough	1893 – 1894

On January 26, 1895, the name of the company was changed to Daisy Manufacturing.

H.W. Baker	1895 – 1919
C.H. Bennett	1920 – 1956
Edward C. Hough	1956 – 1959
Cass S. Hough	1959 – 1971
Richard I. Daniel	1972 – 1983
Cass S. Hough	1983 – 1986
Raymond W. Pilgrim	1987
Marvin Griffin	1988 – 1998
Adam J. Blalock	1998 – 2001
L. Ray Hobbs	2001 – Present

Chronology of Ownership
Over its 125-year history, Daisy has incurred a surprisingly limited number of changes in ownership.

1882 Plymouth Iron Windmill Company
The Plymouth Iron Windmill Company was founded, in 1882, by a group of Plymouth, Michigan, businessmen. The first meeting, held to consider the forming of an association, was attended by M. Conner, L.C. Hough, H.W. Baker, John Bradner, D.G. Bradner, Willard Eldred, D.D. Allen, Myron Gates, Jacob Westfall, J.S. Miller, John Shaw, O.R. Pattingill, L.A. Briggs, O.A. Fraser, Mr. Pinckney, Mr. Chaffee, R.L. Root, C.J. Hamilton and W.O. Allen. At the meeting of the association to discuss forming a company to sell the "Hamilton Iron Wind-mill," Directors electing to purchase stock included R.L. Root, M. Conner, L.C. Hough, S.J. Springer, D.D. Allen, O.R. Pattingill and H.W. Baker.

January 9, 1890, Charles H. Bennett, nephew of Chairman Henry W. Baker, was hired as the company's first salesman of windmills and BB guns. January 11, 1893, Edward C. Hough, son of Lewis C. Hough, was hired as bookkeeper. The Bennett and Hough families would, for years, play important roles in Daisy's growth and success.

1895 Resolution to Change the Company's Name
On January 26, 1895, at a meeting of the board at the office of L.C. Hough, General Manager of the Plymouth Iron Windmill Company, T.C. Sherwood offered a resolution to change the name of the company to Daisy Manufacturing Company. The board, including H.W. Baker, T.C. Sherwood, L.C. Hough and C.J. Hamilton, voted unanimously to change the name.

At the annual stockholders meeting held December 31, 1895, there were 240 shares of stock of Daisy Manufacturing held by:

C.J. Hamilton	80
L.C. Hough	65
E.C. Hough	10
C.H. Bennett	40
O.A. Fraser	10
J.G. Bradner	15
H.W. Baker	10
D.D. Allen	10

1895 - 1960 The Bennett and Hough Era
On the passing of Mr. Baker, Charles H. Bennett became President and Edward C. Hough became Vice President on January 13, 1920. As other investors retired, Hough and Bennett became majority owners. By 1940 each of them held forty-five percent of the company's stock. Daisy Manufacturing Company remained privately owned, primarily by members of the Hough and Bennett families.

Charles H. Bennett passed away September 11, 1956. Bennett's estate was placed in a blood-line trust for Ms. Dede Peck, his niece, and subsequently for Ms. Lyons, his great niece, and subsequently, her descendants. Ms. Peck had lived with Mr. Bennett when she attended high school in order to be near and make regular visits to an orthodontist in Ypsilanti, Michigan. In his later years, she was Mr. Bennett's caretaker.

Edward C. Hough passed away January 24, 1959. On his death, his son Cass Hough inherited his stock.

Both Ms. Peck and Mr. Hough were assessed a large amount of estate taxes and turned to Daisy Manufacturing Company to loan them the money to pay the taxes. It is likely that this debt led Peck and Hough, majority stockholders, to consider a sale of Daisy.

1959 - 1967 Murchison Brothers

Murchison Brothers, an insurance and investment firm, already owned James Heddon's Sons Company (fishing rods and lures), acquired Daisy and merged the two companies to create D & H Corporation (Daisy & Heddon) and a joint sales company, Daisy – Heddon. Cass Hough was a minority investor in that company.

1965 Public Stock Offering

According to Securities and Exchange Commission File 2-23323, Daisy Manufacturing Company registered 200,000 outstanding shares of common stock to be offered for sale to the public by present share holders.

1967 - 1977 Victor Comptometer / Victor Recreation Group

Victor Comptometer acquired Daisy Manufacturing Company and parent company D & H Corporation (Daisy & Heddon), at which point Daisy became Daisy Division Victor Comptometer Corporation. Victor holdings included Burke Golf Equipment Corporation

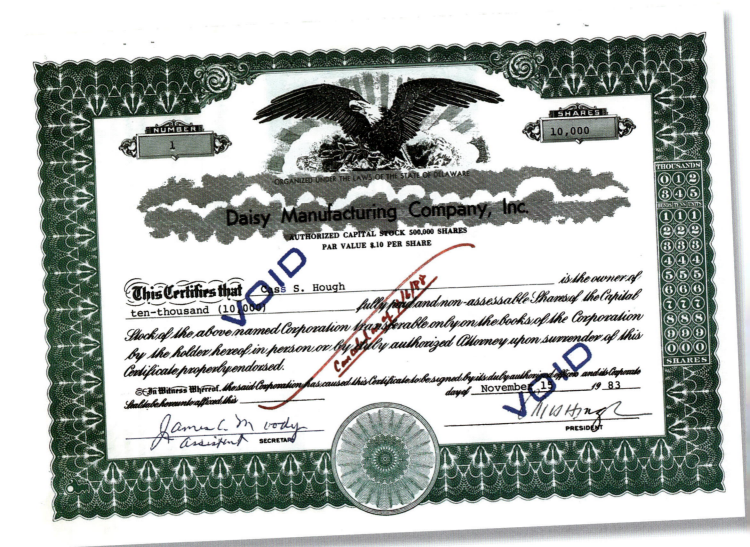

(PGA Golf) and Worthington (golf) Ball Company. Cass Hough stepped down as President of Daisy on July 1, 1972, handing the reins of Daisy over to Dick Daniel. Hough became President of Victor Recreation Group and the group continued to acquire other companies in the lifetime sports category including Ertl Toys, Valley Manufacturing and Sales, Nissen Gymnastics, and Bear Archery. January 1, 1975, Hough resigned as president of Victor Recreation Group but remained on the board.

1977 - 1983 Kidde & Company
Victor Comptometer Corporation became Victor United, Inc.. July 15, 1977, Walter Kidde & Company, Incorporated acquired Victor United, Inc., including the Daisy Division, as a subsidiary of Kidde. In 1979 Walter Kidde & Co., Inc. became Kidde, Inc..

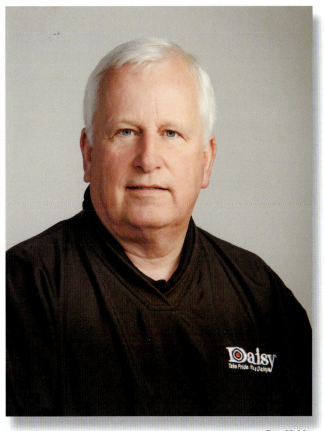
Ray Hobbs

1983 - 1993 Daisy Manufacturing Company, Inc.
Kidde Inc. had been acquired by Hanson Industries, the U.S. arm of Hanson Trust of the United Kingdom. Not interested in all of Kidde's holdings, especially sporting goods companies PGA, Valley, Nissen, Bear and Daisy, Hanson offered those companies for sale.

November 15, 1983, Daisy Manufacturing Co., Inc. was formed when Stephens Inc., investment bankers, assembled a group of private investors to acquire Daisy from Kidde & Company.

Cass Hough returned as President of Daisy and remained President through the company's centennial year, 1986, as he had wished.

1993 - Present Charter Oak Capital Partners
Charter Oak Capital Partners, a private equity firm, acquired Daisy on June 30, 1993. Ray Hobbs, Daisy's President & C.E.O. and Chairman of the Board of Directors, is the company's largest minority owner. A limited number of shares of stock are held by other company officers.

Daisy's Extended Family
There are two young men whom the company considers honorary members of the Daisy Family. They are Rockford Reaume and Fred Gaynor. The Daisy Museum archives house a wealth of antique Daisy advertising. Certainly two of the most significant and most often used images are those of Rockford Reaume, the Happy Daisy Boy, and Frederic John Gaynor, the American Boy's Bill of Rights boy.

In his book *It's a Daisy!*, Cass Hough identified a photo of a young boy with the cut line, "For 20 years, this young Detroit boy, George Rockford, presented Daisy products to American youth – in advertising and on display racks." The company often refers to this young boy as The Happy Daisy Boy. He was clean-cut, good looking and exemplified the wholesome appearance of a young Daisy customer.

In the archives of the Daisy Museum are a set of black and white photos of him with a group of boys holding Daisy guns. The photos, commissioned by Daisy through a Detroit ad agency, were taken at an outdoor commercial photo shoot in 1913. Throughout Daisy's history, the Happy Daisy Boy's image was resurrected many times in advertising. Even today, the image serves as the basis for the logo of the Daisy Airgun Museum.

In September 2005 Tom Reaume contacted Daisy and told the company a wonderful story about his father, Rockford Reaume, being The Happy Daisy Boy. He related that a framed copy of the 1913 Daisy ad, featuring his father as The Happy Daisy Boy had always hung on the wall of their family room. When questioned, Tom had no idea where Cass had come up with the name George Rockford but clarified that his father's name was Rockford Aloysius Reaume. The name Rockford was, in fact, his father's mother's maiden name. (His mother was born in 1898 and it was not uncommon in those days to adopt a mother's maiden name in naming a child.)

Rockford Reaume lived in Grosse Isle, Michigan, and it was there, Tom believed, that his father and a

group of friends were approached by somebody from Daisy to be in a photo shoot for a Daisy marketing promotion. Tom had no knowledge of his father ever being a professional model.

Tom generously supplied the Daisy Museum with a complete set of photos from the 1913 photo shoot. In appreciation, Daisy created a Happy Daisy Boy family tree certificate for each member of the Reaume family and supplied the family with custom Red Ryder BB guns that Christmas.

41

The second young man whose influence on Daisy would warrant induction into the honorary Daisy Family is the late Frederic Gaynor. Frederic Gaynor was the wholesome red haired boy who posed for a photo which became the artwork used for Daisy's American Boy's Bill of Rights. Cass Hough wrote the American Boy's Bill of Rights in 1947, and over two million copies were distributed by Daisy. The image was originally produced as an oil painting. Painted by Walter Parke, it now hangs in the Daisy Museum.

On February 14, 2006, the company was contacted by a friend of Fred's who reported that Fred was currently living south of Paris, France, but coming to the United States to visit family in March. While schedules didn't allow a meeting, Daisy sent a poster, tin sign and coffee mugs, all bearing Fred's childhood likeness, to his brother's home where he would be visiting.

While in France, Fred called Daisy and, within days, emailed a wonderful story about how he

Date: March 27, 2006
Subject: American Boy's Bill of Rights

Many thanks for the Daisy mementos --

   That was kind and considerate of you. Not having lived in the U.S. for the past 25 years, I had no idea the Daisy ad I posed for in 1947 at the age of 12 was still so prolific. As I recall, it was primarily featured on the back covers of comic books and "Boys Life" magazine. My mother sent away for one poster which I still have and which has traveled with me to 11 foreign postings as a U.S. Embassy Foreign Service officer in Africa and Asia. I retired in 2000 and currently live in Perpignan, France, with my wife Susan.
   At the age of three, my parents registered me with the Chicago-based Models Bureau located on Wacker Drive. It was owned and operated by Connie and Al Seaman. Registering with the Models Bureau was the result of a free lance photographer shooting me -- age 3 holding a football entitled, "Aspirations" -- winning the First Prize of 1,000 British Pounds in the 1938 Kodak UK Photo Contest. The photographer, who won that prize and money, was Mr. Nowell Ward of Chicago. It was he who encouraged my parents for me to become a professional model.
   My memory may be a bit hazy, but I do remember going to photo shoots in and around the Chicago area during my grammar school days and into high school. My mother tried to save samples from all my jobs, and they number into the hundreds. The Daisy ad took place during the sunset days of my modeling career. I believe the ad was created by the Sundblom Studios in Chicago. I remember having worked for the Sundblom Studios in the Coca-Cola "Family Series" in the early to mid forties. I believe it was the Sundblom people who selected me for the Daisy ad. It was a school day...and as my principal liked my parents, she allowed me generous time-off from attending classes.
   I remember doing three or four different poses. Incidentally, the wrist watch on my left hand was my father's watch. My wife still wears that watch today. The shirt was a hand-me-down from older brother. The short sleeved sweater and jeans were mine. My hair was not really that curly. At the end of the shoot, the producer offered me a Daisy BB gun (which I really wanted) -- but, my mother declined. Curiously, while in basic training with the US Army after graduating Beloit College in 1957, I was one of only three marksmen out of 150 soldiers in my training group at Ft. Carson, Colorado. I have never had the opportunity to show my marksmanship again.
   Joe, I hope this will be of interest to you. Thanks again for helping me to recall fond memories of my association with Daisy.

   Best regards,
   Frederic J. Gaynor

happened to pose for the image which became The American Boy's Bill of Rights poster.

Mr. Gaynor is most likely correct about recalling posing at Haddon Sundblom's Studio in Chicago for the Daisy photo. Fred had been born in Chicago, where his parents registered him with the Chicago-based Models Bureau at an early age. He appeared in ads for Coca-Cola, Borden's Milk, 7 UP, Daisy and hundreds of other products.

Sundblom is best known for illustrating Coca-Cola's Santa Claus images. He was born in Chicago and worked at other studios before opening his own in the mid-1920s when he began producing advertising for D'Arcy Advertising Agency's client Coca-Cola. Walter Parke, who painted the oil painting from photos of Fred Gaynor, was born in Little Rock, Arkansas, in 1909 and studied at the Art Institute of Chicago. Research indicates that he was a student of Sundblom and, it's likely, an artist for hire with or commissioned by the Sundblom Studio.

Mr. Gaynor graduated Beloit College in Wisconsin, with a degree in theater and government in 1957. After serving in the U.S. Army in France, he joined the Foreign Service. He served with the United States Information Agency in ten African countries and then in Vietnam with the Commerce Department's U.S. and Foreign Commercial Service. He retired in 1999 and moved to Sarasota, Florida, in 2007.

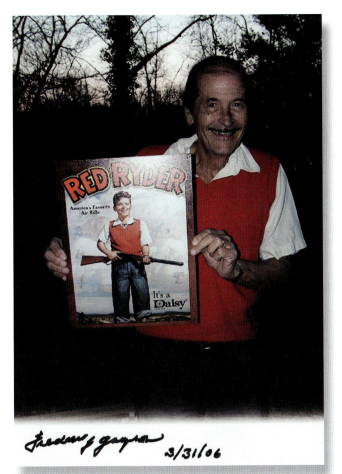

The week of March 23, 2009, Daisy received a phone call from the friend of Fred Gaynor who had re-introduced the company to him in 2006. He reported that Fred was in hospice care. Daisy responded by over-nighting a package containing several products bearing Fred's boyhood likeness, including a poster which was signed by many Daisy employees. Frederic J. Gaynor passed away March 29, 2009.

Homecoming Celebration
Fifty Years in Rogers, Arkansas

In 2008, on the occasion of Daisy's fiftieth year in Rogers, Arkansas, the company hosted a Homecoming for its Daisy Family of employees, retirees, Friends of the Daisy Museum and Daisy collectors at the John Q. Hammons Convention Center. The Homecoming event was held June 19 through 22, 2008, almost exactly coinciding with the fiftieth anniversary of the production of the first Daisy airgun in Rogers on June 26, 1958.

The event was a tremendous success and no one went home empty handed. Some collectors took home an antique Daisy or a limited edition Daisy for their collection. Retirees took home a candy bowl or T-shirt to commemorate the event. Some took home rare items they bought in the silent auction. Most took home new friendships, great memories and a better sense for what it means to be a part of the Daisy Family.

CHAPTER 7
AT HOME IN ROGERS

Daisy Put Rogers, Arkansas, on the Map
Daisy feels at home in Rogers, Arkansas. After all, the company has maintained corporate offices here since 1958 and remains involved in the community. Just about everyone in Northwest Arkansas has a relative or knows someone who once worked for Daisy. While certainly not the largest employer in the region, Daisy is one of the most recognized companies in Northwest Arkansas. Since 1958, when the company moved to Rogers from Plymouth, Michigan, the company has stamped the address Rogers, Arkansas, into millions of products.

While Daisy has had only two corporate headquarters - Plymouth, Michigan, and Rogers, Arkansas - it has maintained other offices and manufactured or assembled products at other locations.

Fifth Avenue, New York
In 1937 Daisy marketed a wide array of toy guns, pop guns and water guns. With the addition of the Buck Rogers line, Daisy and All Metal Products Company jointly opened an office in New York's Toy Center at 200 Fifth Avenue in Manhattan on February 6, 1938. It was All Metal Products which had ten years earlier bought BB gun tooling from Sears Roebuck & Company. The offices were originally occupied by Daisy's Cass Hough and All Metal Products' Vice President and Sales Manager, Bill Wenner on a part time basis. Bill would later join Daisy's sales force to help develop the toy segment. In 1942 Reg Lockwood would office there and eventually Ertl Toys would market both die cast toys and Daisy toy guns from that office.

Preston, Ontario, Canada
April 6, 1958, Daisy of Canada, LTD was established with Norman Golightly serving as President and General Manager of the plant in Preston, a community in Cambridge, Ontario. Daisy shared the facility with another company owned by Golightly which made holsters and sourced toy cap pistols.

In 1961 Daisy and Heddon maintained a manufacturing operation in the former Preston Furniture factory at 185 King Street E., where they established an indoor shooting range. In 1968 – 1969 the operation was moved to 866 Langs Drive. Shortly after Daisy-Heddon

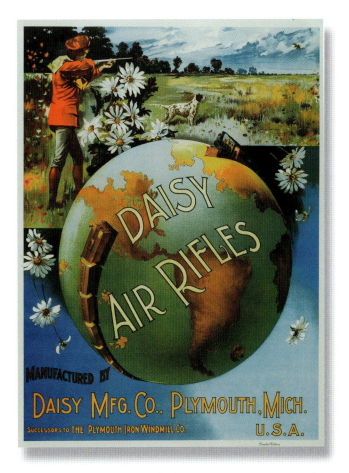

became a subsidiary of Victor Comptometer Ltd., they relocated in order to share manufacturing space at Victor Comptometer's factory at 55 Savage Drive.

Daisy was exporting BBs to Canada and, to reduce freight costs, began manufacturing BBs at the Preston plant. Daisy of Canada also did some final assembly of airguns and handled European sales. Later, when mis-shapen BBs were found in Europe, the BBs were replaced by Daisy's Rogers, Arkansas, facility and the Canadian facility was shut down.

India
Although ground was broken for the construction of a Daisy production facility in Chandigarh, Punjab, India, on January 26, 1964, the plant was never opened. Under British rule, ownership of

guns by natives had been forbidden. Following the decolonization, the government of the State of Punjab was convinced by Daisy's Cass Hough that the future capabilities of their armed forces would benefit from a BB gun marksmanship training program in the schools.

Dick Daniel, Vice President of Manufacturing, specified necessary tools and machinery and drew up plans for an impressive manufacturing facility. Cass Hough traveled to India on several occasions, and the Punjab government selected a site for the plant. A three-step plan to first market Daisy guns, then assemble them and finally manufacture them on site presented tremendous opportunities for Daisy, for the State of Punjab and for the workforce. When it was discovered that the plant did not have access to water and when the Chief Minister, who was supporting this project for his government, was assassinated in February 1965 the project was scrapped.

Mexico
Also in the 1960s, in pursuit of a low cost producer, Daisy sent tools to an existing factory in Mexico. After only a short period of production, due to less than satisfactory quality of production, Daisy dissolved its relationship with the Mexican manufacturer. Airguns made in that plant were marketed as being made in Mexico and were distributed only in Mexico and South America and not into the United States.

Becoming an Assembly Operation
In the late 1990s the tooling necessary for the production of many of Daisy's products was aging, and a major investment would be required to refurbish and replace it. In a continuing effort to control costs, improve efficiency and ensure quality, the company began purchasing components from highly specialized manufacturers.

"The Cave"
In 1995 Daisy had acquired Brass Eagle, a Canadian paintball and marker company, in order to offer a complete line of paintball markers. While Daisy Manufacturing Company's corporate headquarters, customer service operations, some assembly operations and BB shot manufacturing remained at the plant at 2111 South Eighth Street in Rogers, Brass Eagle operations were located in an assembly facility in Granby, Missouri. From April 1996 until November 1997 some Daisy products were also assembled in the Granby facility while other production lines remained in Rogers, Arkansas. When the paintball business

became sufficient to stand alone, the two companies were separated, and stock in Brass Eagle was offered to the public in November 1997.

As an assembly operation, Daisy no longer had need for the expansive manufacturing facility on Eighth Street in Rogers. The property was listed for sale and, in April 1997, Daisy had settled on an underground facility on Lime Kiln Road in Neosho, Missouri, which met its needs. The limestone walls of the underground facility provided insulation from outside temperatures and ensured a consistent, moderate climate. The Neosho facility was headquarters not only for assembly operations, but also for purchasing, shipping and receiving, engineering research and development and quality control staff. The corporate offices remained in Rogers.

Salem, Missouri, BB Production Facility
When the Daisy plant on South Eighth Street in Rogers was sold in 1999, the BB production remained at that facility until 2003. For efficiency, Daisy relocated its BB production equipment to Salem, Missouri, to be near a plater. During this time period, the company constantly compared the cost of producing BBs domestically with the cost of purchasing finished BBs from China. For three years Daisy marketed both sourced and domestically produced BBs but was forced to close the Salem, Missouri, BB Production Facility on January 31, 2006.

Relocating Corporate Offices to Stribling Drive
Following the sale of the Eighth Street manufacturing facility, Daisy was allowed to

Brass plated Daisy with medallion inset into a maple stock, made to commemorate the company's 120th anniversary.

remain in the office building, adjacent to the plant, as a tenant for six months. In November 1999 the company moved into new corporate offices at 400 West Stribling Dr., within Magnolia Industrial Park, off of North Second Street, about one mile north of downtown Rogers. While leaving the old facility was emotional for those who had worked in the plant for years, the antiquated brick and concrete block office building had offered no room for expansion and was less than accommodating for current technology. The new 10,000 square

Raymond Burns, President / C.E.O., Rogers-Lowell Area Chamber of Commerce and Ray Hobbs present an engraved Red Ryder to then Rogers Mayor Steve Womack.

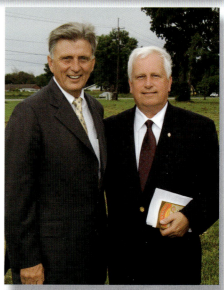

Arkansas Governor Mike Beebe with Daisy President & C.E.O. Ray Hobbs.

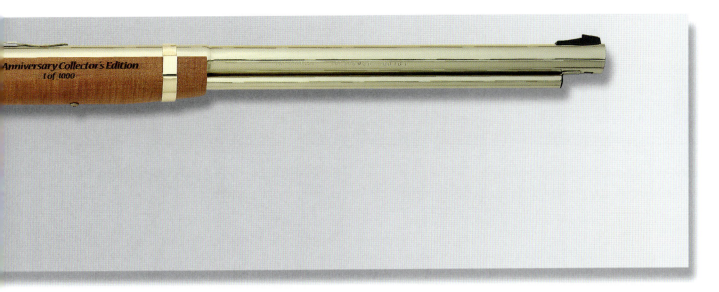

foot office space featured an open atrium with a conference room and adequate office space for the company's administrative, sales, engineering, information services and customer service staff as well as for future expansion needs.

Homecoming

In 2006 Daisy celebrated its 120th anniversary. In May 2007 the antique Daisy neon sign was restored and re-erected at the southwest corner of Stribling and Second Streets, in front of the company's offices in Rogers. Following that ceremony, Daisy President & C.E.O. Ray Hobbs huddled at the base of the old sign with Raymond Burns, President / C.E.O. of the Rogers-Lowell Chamber of Commerce and Rogers Mayor Steve Womack.

Within twenty-four hours, a meeting was held with the Arkansas Industrial Development Commission in order to let Governor Mike Beebe know of the company's intent to bring its assembly back to Rogers, Arkansas.

On June 20, 2007, Ray Hobbs and Governor Beebe made an announcement at a press conference held under a tent in the field in front of Daisy's offices: Daisy is coming home to Rogers. After ten years of assembly operations in Neosho, Missouri, Daisy would relocate the entire operations under one roof, in the same facility in which the company had housed their offices since November 1999. The move was made in record time. While the company had planned on being in production in early August, the first Red Ryder came off the production line on July 25, 2007.

In 2008 Daisy celebrated fifty years in Rogers, Arkansas. The City of Rogers and Daisy hosted a four-day weekend Homecoming. In addition to Daisy staff, Daisy Museum personnel, retirees and community friends, 189 Daisy collectors from every corner of the U.S. and Canada, registered for the event. An extremely limited edition engraved Red Ryder BB gun commemorated the event and was numbered 1 of 189 corresponding to the 189 people who registered for the event and reserved one of the guns.

The ticketed event began with a Rogers-Lowell Chamber of Commerce reception under a tent in front of the Daisy offices on Thursday, June 19th. Tours of the Daisy Museum and the Daisy assembly operation were offered throughout the weekend. On Friday afternoon, a picnic was hosted by Daisy, and it was Daisy Night at the Northwest Arkansas Naturals baseball game.

Saturday, exhibitors displayed and enjoyed a swap meet at the John Q. Hammons Convention Center, adjacent to the Embassy Suites host hotel. On-site appraisals were offered. An activity called Speed Daisy allowed registrants to visit with current Daisy staff and retirees to hear their personal Daisy stories.

Saturday evening began with a reception and silent auction, filled with unique one-of-a-kind prototype Daisy items and other amazing collectibles donated by those who registered. The group was entertained by "Melody

Wild Goose Pottery of Arkansas was commissioned to produce a 50 Years in Rogers candy dish for the occasion.

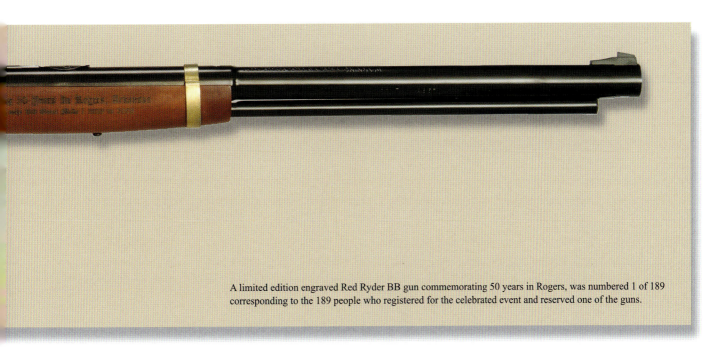

A limited edition engraved Red Ryder BB gun commemorating 50 years in Rogers, was numbered 1 of 189 corresponding to the 189 people who registered for the celebrated event and reserved one of the guns.

Lane," a barbershop quartet that sang custom lyrics to the tune of "A Bicycle Built for Two" (a.k.a. "Daisy, Daisy…"). The program included a welcome from Ray Hobbs and Rogers Mayor Steve Womack. The Daisy Museum accepted a significant donation of Quick Kill material from the family of Mike Jennings, which had been coordinated by Daisy collector Dave Albert. The Daisy Museum introduced a limited edition 25th anniversary Christmas gun and Daisy showed a prototype and officially announced its commitment to replicate the first wirestock Daisy BB gun.

Taking Pride

The late David Gates, long-time Daisy executive and curator of the Daisy Museum had a favorite quote, attributable to President Abraham Lincoln,

"I like to see a man proud of the place he lives. I like to see a man live so that his place will be proud of him."

Daisy has always been a good, yet humble, corporate citizen. The following are just a few examples of the company's involvement and investment in the betterment of the communities in which the Daisy Family lives and works:

Open Avenues

(formerly the Adult Development Center) provides transportation, daily living skills training and job skills training to adults with disabilities. For several years, Daisy has been

a corporate sponsor of the organization and a contributor to its building campaign. The Workshop at Open Avenues provides income-producing opportunities for its clients while offering local industry an opportunity to access a dedicated and conscientious workforce. Daisy is proud to support Open Avenues by utilizing their capable clientele to package BBs, paint safeties, package and label product and prepare literature packets.

The Benton County Sunshine School serves infants to three year olds with developmental disabilities. The curriculum includes social and living skills components as well as elements of primary education in both classroom settings and on an individual basis. Speech, occupational and physical therapy

are also available. When the Sunshine School outgrew its facility, it approached local industry for funding to construct one which would meet current needs and provide opportunity to extend the effective future reach of their services. Daisy was pleased to provide funding to assist in building a new 40,000 square foot facility, enabling the school to serve the needs of over five hundred people each year.

Arkansas Children's Hospital is the only Pediatric Level I trauma center in Arkansas, serving patients from birth to age twenty-one, and their families. Because motor vehicle crashes are the leading cause of death for children, each patient must leave the hospital in an appropriate and properly installed car seat.

A gift from Daisy to ACH provided more than one thousand one hundred car seats for patients leaving the hospital, regardless of their family's ability to pay.

United Way of Northwest Arkansas is dedicated to improving lives through advancement of programs that enhance education, income and health. For a number of years, the Daisy Family chose, as a group, to support this organization through payroll deductions.

Employees also donated their skills and time to work at select United Way agencies during the National Day of Caring. Daisy's corporate pledge, coupled with the results of creative fundraising efforts, earned the company recognition for its per capita contribution.

Rebuilding Together of Northwest Arkansas is an organization in which several members of the Daisy Family actively participate. The non-profit, locally-funded organization assembles a volunteer workforce to assist local residents with

home improvement projects. The team helps the elderly, disabled persons, single parents and those who are financially challenged, partnering with friends and family to clean, paint and make home improvements. Rebuilding Together is an excellent example of the Daisy Family members

at work to improve the communities in which they live.

Not surprisingly, Daisy is a company recognized for excellence in the workplace. In 2009 Daisy was the recipient of an Arkansas Governor's Workplace Award based on performance excellence. The application process utilized the Malcolm Baldrige Criteria to assess the company's leadership, strategic planning, customer and market focus, measurement analysis and knowledge management, human resource focus, process management and results. Daisy's application highlighted the company's management techniques and dedication to helping staff balance work and life.

Through Daisy's generosity and the generosity of the Daisy Family, children's lives are protected, youth recreational opportunities are enhanced, homes are improved, special needs are met and those less privileged can, with dignity, take pride in their accomplishments.

Chapter 8

Teaching America to Shoot

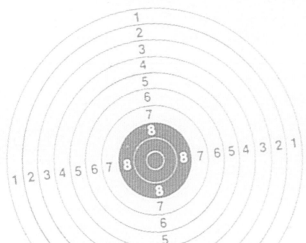

Daisy is the Leader in Shooting Education

No company has helped teach more Americans to shoot than has Daisy. There is little doubt that most people who have grown up shooting firearms took their first shot with a Daisy BB gun. Because training is one of the primary uses of airguns and because Daisy is the leading manufacturer of airguns, the company has always taken seriously its obligation to emphasize shooting safety.

Airguns Have Historically Been Used for Training

Mechanical airguns have been around since about 1580. The category has a proven history of being a useful tool for small game hunting, target practice, formal match competition and training. According to Jess Galan, a retired certified police firearms instructor, forensic firearms examiner, contributing author to several firearms and shooting magazines and author of *Airgun*

Digest, air guns have many uses. "Airguns are utilized primarily for training. First-time firearm shooters often purchase an airgun in order to familiarize themselves with the feel and function of a comparable firearm," states Galan. "Not only do young shooters learn marksmanship skills; they learn discipline, self-control, patience, respect for others' property and personal responsibility."

Almost Anyone; Almost Anywhere

Being able to shoot an airgun in a backyard or even in a basement, with a proper trap and backstop, offers convenience, extends the shooting season and offers substantial cost savings compared with firearms range fees and high ammunition cost.

Airgun shooting is a very personal sport. It challenges the individual, tests personal motivation, hones the senses and focuses concentration. Participants don't have to be athletic to excel. Size, speed, age, and strength are not requirements for a shooter's success. It simply takes concentration, discipline and determination.

Airgun shooters can compete in Sporter and Precision category competitions and even earn NCAA scholarships. Because the mainstream media typically doesn't cover the events, few people are aware that airgun competition has been an official Olympic Sport since 1984.

The Daisy Shooting Education Program

A lot of credit for Daisy's formal shooting education program is given to David Gates, as well it should be. However, the truth is, there were serious efforts by the company to create educational partnerships with local schools and other organizations as early as 1948.

It was at the end of the school year in

10 SHOOTING SAFETY RULES

1. Always keep the muzzle pointed in a safe direction.
There are several safe "carries" depending on the situation. Never allow the muzzle to point in the direction of a person.

2. Treat every gun as if it were loaded.
You can never be positive that you were the last person to handle the gun. Never take anyone's word about whether or not a gun is loaded. Always check a gun to see if it is loaded when removed from storage or received from another person. Even if you have fired an airgun one or more times and no pellet or BB was expelled from the barrel, it does not mean that the magazine of the gun is empty of ammunition. Any airgun can fail to feed for any number of reasons. Continue to treat the airgun as loaded and ready to fire. Always treat a gun as if it is loaded even if you know it isn't.

3. Only load or cock a gun when you are shooting.
A loaded gun has no place in your home or other public place.

4. Check your target and beyond your target.
Be sure all persons are well clear of the target area before you shoot. Check behind and beyond your target to be certain you have a safe backstop and that no person or property could be endangered.

5. Anyone shooting or near a shooter should wear shooting glasses.
Also, all other persons should remain behind the shooter.

6. Never climb or jump with a gun.
You can't control the direction of the muzzle if you stumble or fall. You should safely lay the gun down or hand it to a companion while you climb or jump over anything.

7. Avoid ricochet.
Never shoot at a flat hard surface or at the surface of water. Ammunition can ricochet off of water just like a skipped rock.

8. Keep the muzzle clear.
Never let anything obstruct the muzzle of a gun. Don't allow the muzzle to come in contact with the ground.

9. Guns not in use should always be unloaded.
Keeping guns unloaded when not in use is critical to the safety of you and others. When you are finished shooting, put the trigger safety in the "on" position and unload the gun. Store guns so that they are inaccessible to untrained shooters and store ammunition separately from the gun.

10. Respect other people's property.
Whether you're target shooting or hunting, if you're a guest on others' land, you should leave it exactly as you found it.

1956 that David Gates, a coach in the Detroit, Michigan, public school system, agreed to take on a special project for Daisy. Dave was hired specifically to establish and grow a formal shooting education program for Daisy. David set up the Training Services Department and worked with the American Alliance for Health, Physical Education and Recreation to make target shooting with BB guns a part of schools' physical education curriculum. He made contact with Dr. Julian Smith, with the University of Michigan, who had worked with schools in the upper Midwest in the area of lifetime sports, a program which included shooting, archery, fishing and orienteering.

When Daisy moved to Rogers, Arkansas, in 1958, David assumed the responsibility of product development. Incidentally, David Gates went on to serve Daisy in the marketing and public relations departments, served on the Rogers Public Schools Board of Directors, retired from Daisy and worked at the Daisy Museum from 2000 until shortly before his passing in 2005.

Jack Reid (who had a background in education as well) was hired to manage the shooting education programs for the company. Daisy had established a shooting education program in Rogers, Arkansas, at the Armory. Rogers Junior Chamber (Jaycees) members Mike Rizzuti, Jack Marshall, head of the National Guard Armory, "Junior" Creech, a local postman as well as Jim Sawyer, Jim Clark, Chuck Basse and Orin Ribar of Daisy participated in the program, teaching gun safety and marksmanship skills. Jack Reid was working with Jack Powers and approached this Jaycees chapter about presenting their model local program at the Arkansas State Jaycees convention at the Arlington Hotel in Hot Springs, Arkansas.

Jack Reid equipped Chuck Basse and Jim Sawyer with the equipment they would require to set up a shooting range and demonstrate the education program in Hot Springs. Based on the positive response, Reid and Powers, accompanied by Homer Circle, then Daisy's VP for Advertising, called on the Arkansas Jaycees organization in Little Rock and then the national headquarters of the Jaycees organization in Tulsa, Oklahoma, proposing that the Jaycees adopt the program on a national basis.

The educational part of the curriculum was implemented regionally at first, in neighboring states of Oklahoma, Kansas and Missouri, before the program was adopted nationally. It would be several years before a competitive element was added to the program. Daisy's participation with the Jaycees became the longest running corporate partnership in their history. Jack Reid ultimately returned to the field of education as a science teacher in the Rogers Public Schools.

Ten Lesson Curriculum
When it comes to shooting education and training, Daisy literally wrote the book. Daisy quickly recognized the need for a written curriculum. Bob Goss, whose background with Winchester included shooting education, was hired to head the program. He also had been a physical education teacher and a coach, involved as an instructor in lifetime sports. Bob worked with the Missouri Department of Game and Fish to develop a written curriculum and was instrumental in working with 4-H in

the development of the airgun segment of their overall hunting education and shooting sports program.

With minor evolution, that curriculum continues to be used by most shooting education programs today. Daisy's *Ten Lesson Curriculum for Shooting Education* not only provides the lessons for an instructor to present to the student, but also provides the instructor with lesson goals, personnel requirements and materials needs.

Tom Louks, assistant principal at Rogers High School, was hired by Daisy to work with Bob Goss and ultimately took over the shooting education program.

John Ford was also the assistant principal at Rogers High School when he was hired by Jack Powers in 1974, initially as a temporary employee for the summer to assist with public relations. John remained with Daisy for thirty years, working primarily in marketing, advertising, public relations and sales. It was only when Tom Louks left the company that John assumed the responsibility of managing the shooting education program.

Hundreds of thousands of young people have been introduced to shooting safety through Daisy's ten-lesson classroom curriculum and practical instruction from volunteers. In addition to the Junior Chamber, Daisy has worked closely with 4-H Shooting Sports, American Legion, the National Rifle Association, National Guard Youth Marksmanship Program, USA Shooting, Cadet Leagues of Canada, Royal Rangers, the International Hunter Education Association, churches, camps and civic and conservation organizations to make instructional material and equipment available.

On the Road to the Daisy Nationals

Most successful recreational education programs involve a competitive element, and the shooting sports are no different. It has been proven that young people will remain involved in a program for a longer period of time if there is an opportunity to compete and to be recognized or rewarded.

The youngest athletes shoot BB guns in four positions (standing, sitting, kneeling and prone) at a five meter distance. Daisy's Model 499 AVANTI Champion, a descendant of the Model 99, is billed as the world's most accurate BB

gun and is the only gun approved for the Daisy Nationals five meter competition.

Older athletes shoot Sporter classification pellet rifles in three positions (often referred to as 3-P) including prone, standing and kneeling at a ten meter distance. Sporter classification rifles include single pump pneumatic rifles such as Daisy's Model 853 AVANTI Legend, Model 753 AVANTI Elite, refillable CO_2 models such as Daisy's Model 888 AVANTI Medalist and Model 887 Gold Medalist as well as pre-charged (compressed air) rifles. The AVANTI name, an Italian word meaning go ahead or step forward, was chosen by Daisy in 2000 as a brand for the company's training and match competition guns.

Each of the groups with whom Daisy works shares the company's passion for teaching young

Model 499 AVANTI Champion

Model 853 AVANTI Legend

Model 888 AVANTI Medalist

Model 887 AVANTI Gold Medalist

people how to shoot safely. Dedicated coaches recruit interested young people to attend their class, where the *Daisy Ten Lesson Curriculum* is presented in a classroom setting. It is not until after the curriculum has been completed that a coach will take the team onto the range to shoot. The most promising shooters will comprise a competitive five meter BB gun team that will practice throughout the season. Teams compete in state matches, typically sanctioned by the National Rifle Association or 4-H Shooting Sports. The top three teams in each state match qualify to compete in the Daisy National BB Gun Championship Match (The Daisy Nationals), once titled the International BB Gun Championship Match (IBBGCM).

The first national match was held in 1966 and has been held at shooting facilities, Olympic facilities and colleges all over the country. Over the forty-six year history, the match has attracted teams from every state plus the District of Columbia.

Daisy National BB Gun Championship Match Locations

Year	Location
1966	Dayton, Ohio
1967	Hutchinson, Kansas
1968	Irving, Texas
1969	Overland Park, Kansas
1970	Irving, Texas
1971	Merritt Island, Florida
1972	Tulsa, Oklahoma
1973	Phoenix, Arizona
1974	Manchester, New Hampshire
1975	Clarksville, Tennessee
1976	Shreveport, Louisiana
1977	Sioux Falls, South Dakota
1978	Dubuque, Iowa
1979	Joplin, Missouri
1980	Bowling Green, Kentucky
1981	Sioux Falls, South Dakota
1982	Clarksville, Tennessee
1983	Bowling Green, Kentucky
1984	Fayetteville, Arkansas
1985	Slippery Rock, Pennsylvania
1986	Bowling Green, Kentucky
1987	Gorham, Maine
1988	Colorado Springs, Colorado
1989	Tulsa, Oklahoma
1990	Tulsa, Oklahoma
1991	Bowling Green, Kentucky
1992	Bowling Green, Kentucky
1993	Bowling Green, Kentucky
1994	Bowling Green, Kentucky
1995	Bowling Green, Kentucky
1996	Bowling Green, Kentucky
1997	Bowling Green, Kentucky
1998	Manhattan, Kansas
1999	Atlanta, Georgia
2000	Atlanta, Georgia
2001	Colorado Springs, Colorado
2002	Atlanta, Georgia
2003	Wilmington, North Carolina
2004	Bowling Green, Kentucky
2005	Bowling Green, Kentucky
2006	Bowling Green, Kentucky
2007	Bowling Green, Kentucky
2008	Bowling Green, Kentucky
2009	Bowling Green, Kentucky
2010	Rogers, Arkansas
2011	Rogers, Arkansas

Bringing the Daisy Nationals to Daisy's Hometown

In 2010, for the first time in 45 years, Daisy's staff and the City of Rogers were able to work together to attract and host the match over the July 4th weekend. Being able to host the match

in the company's hometown allows Daisy to offer tours of the factory and of the Daisy Museum, host a picnic and enjoy a baseball game together.

Forty-three teams, representing eighteen states, competed in the match in 2010 and the company's goal is to continually grow those numbers.

A score on a written safety test, based on the *Daisy Ten Lesson Curriculum*, is combined with each shooter's target scores. Often the safety test score will be the determining factor in a close competition.

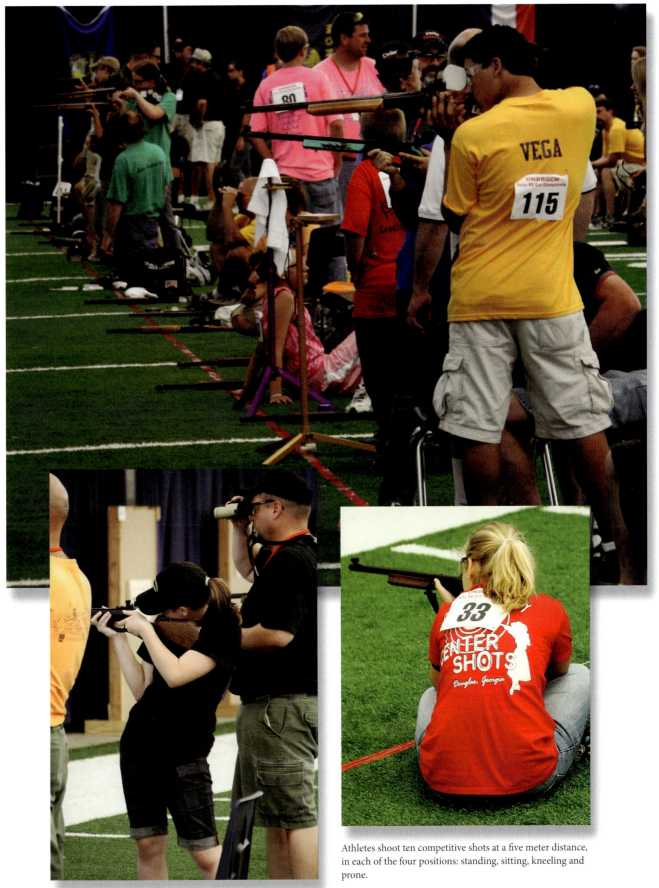

Athletes shoot ten competitive shots at a five meter distance, in each of the four positions: standing, sitting, kneeling and prone.

Participation in the match and related activities is limited to those teams who qualify and register for the event. However, spectators are welcomed at the match. The Daisy Nationals represent the best of the best young athletes and the tip of the iceberg when it comes to match competition.

Teams are comprised of five athletes and two alternates. Several of the coaches who bring a team to this match have been coaching for twenty to thirty years, and one coach attending has qualified to bring a team to this national match for twenty-five consecutive years.

At the opening ceremonies, athletes assemble, wearing their team colors and carrying their state flag. The young competitors are, for the most part, accompanied by parents and siblings who turn the event into a family vacation.

While competitors and their coaches are focused on the match itself, there is always time to make new friends and have fun. At the Barter Bar, athletes trade with each other items they have brought from their home state.

For every competitor at the national match, there are thousands who attended a class, learned the shooting safety curriculum and didn't qualify for a team. And there are additional thousands who competed on a team but didn't qualify at a state match.

The Commitment Continues

Today, Daisy's commitment to shooting education and the nation-wide programs which touch the lives of hundreds of thousands of young shooters is greater than ever. In fact, the company's marketing effort remains focused on developing, improving and growing this important program. Today, working with teams and coaches throughout the year, attending state matches and planning for and hosting the Daisy national match requires the efforts of the entire Daisy team.

There are two members of the Daisy Family, however, who deserve special recognition. Denise Johnson has represented the friendly voice, the positive attitude, the corporate ethics and the servant heart of Daisy since 1979. As National Account Manager, she is the company's key contact with the various shooting programs and their coaches. She's affectionately known, by the young athletes at the Daisy Nationals, as Miss Daisy.

There's only one thing that Service Supervisor Raymond Stansell loves to do more than teach kids to shoot and that's to make them smile. Raymond went to work for Daisy in 1972 and has been involved in or responsible for just about every facet of the Daisy Nationals every year since. Raymond's knowledge of the rules and attention to detail ensure that the firing points at the match are set correctly and to specification. In addition to his responsibilities at the match, Raymond typically creates two special Daisy Champion Model 499 BB guns, to be randomly given away to one boy and one girl.

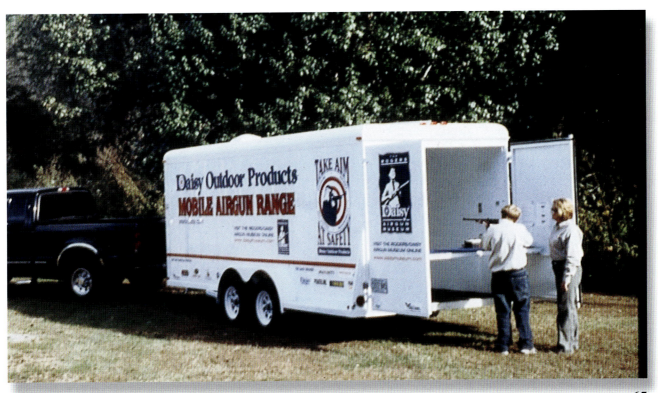

Taking Shooting Education on the Road

While Daisy's national match and structured shooting education program reach hundreds of thousands of young people annually, the company recognizes that not everyone who wants to learn how to shoot wants to compete on a team. In 2002, in order to extend its reach to even more young and first time shooters, Daisy built a Mobile Airgun Range in order to present shooting safety at major outdoor events all over the country. The back doors of the eighteen foot steel trailer open and a shooting bench folds down, creating two firing points, each with an electric target runner. Two Daisy AVANTI Model 888 match competition pellet rifles have been plumbed to accept a continuous flow of CO_2 from a twenty-five pound tank.

In order to reach even more young and first time shooters, Daisy designed and created ten inflatable BB gun ranges and placed them with sales representatives around the country, making it more practical for retail customers and outdoor event organizers to have access to a safe Daisy BB gun range. The inflatable ranges are powered by a small fan and inflate in less than one minute. Layers of ballistic fabric provide a more than adequate backstop for the low velocity BB guns used on these ranges.

In 2007 the Youth Shooting Sports Alliance was formed by a group of leaders in the shooting industry, including a representative from Daisy. YSSA's National Youth Shooting Sports Program Needs Assessment evaluates

and prioritizes shooting sports programs based on their potential program and participation growth. YSSA identifies equipment and supply needs which limit the growth of these top programs then works to find donated, discounted and loaned equipment to help maximize each program's potential reach and effectiveness. Through Daisy's support, the YSSA has helped to introduce thousands of young people to the shooting sports.

Teaching America to Shoot is Daisy's Passion
Daisy is grateful to the parents, mentors, volunteers and coaches who devote their time, energy and resources to teaching young people shooting safety and marksmanship skills. Only with their assistance has it been possible for the company's programs and materials to have touched so many lives.

From the company's first involvement in structured education programs in 1948, through the development of a written curriculum, to the present day sponsorship of the prestigious annual Daisy National BB Gun Championship Match, shooting education has remained an integral part of Daisy's corporate culture. Being the leader in shooting education has been, and remains, Daisy's obligation, honor and passion.

Chapter 9
Defending What's Right

On October 30, 2001, the Consumer Product Safety Commission (CPSC), under the leadership of then Chairwoman Ann Brown, filed an administrative complaint against Daisy, aggressively pursuing a recall of Daisy's high-powered air rifles. The complaint was not based on a product defect but, in fact, a perceived potential misuse. The case would not be resolved until November 14, 2003. For two years and fifteen days the future of Daisy and the future of airguns in general hung in jeopardy.

All Sports Pose Risk
Participation in any sport or recreational activity poses risk of injury. The Consumer Product Safety Commission, through its National Electronic Injury Surveillance System (NEISS), gathers statistics related to injuries associated with consumer products and activities based on data from nationally representative samples of hospital emergency rooms throughout the United States. Year after year, sports such as bicycling, basketball, football and even fishing are responsible for more trips to emergency rooms than is the sport of airgun shooting.

There is no doubt, however, that when misused, carelessly used or criminally used an airgun can cause serious injury or death to the user or those around him. Daisy has been, and remains, dedicated to providing users of its products with the warnings, instructions and information necessary for them to safely enjoy its products.

Daisy Leads the Industry
Daisy has consistently led the product category in establishing and exceeding industry standards for marking airguns and their packaging. For example, it was in 1973, before industry standards even existed, that Daisy first placed age recommendations on its packaging. Similar age recommendations were subsequently adopted by the American Society for Testing and Materials (ASTM) as a part of its standards for non-powder (airgun) categories. In 1974 Dick Daniel, then Vice President of Manufacturing, chaired the first ASTM task group on non-powder guns. Dick drafted what would be published as the first set of standards for non-powder guns and ammunition in 1979. Today, Daisy remains diligent in its compliance with ASTM standards for product

marking and testing, operations manual content, packaging markings and warning language.

At the core of the company's comprehensive Take Aim at Safety program is its policy of placing a copy of the ten shooting safety rules inside the package of every Daisy airgun sold. When followed, these safety rules will avert accidents. If the first rule of shooting safety was always followed (Always keep the muzzle pointed in a safe direction) there would be no injury incidents. Period.

In fact, at the heart of most unfortunate injury incidents involving an airgun is a careless act, reckless and irresponsible misuse, lack of adult supervision and a willing disregard for at least one of the shooting safety rules.

Disregarding the Facts
In their eventual complaint against Daisy, the CPSC took the position that any airgun with a gravity feed loading mechanism that may fail to feed "encourages needless undertaking of risk." They also charged that the guns should have an automatic safety and that BBs are difficult to see in the loading port. It is important to note that the CPSC had reviewed these same models several times over the past twenty years and always found them to be safe and free of defect.

Disregarding the facts of these previous findings, then outgoing CPSC Chairwoman Ann Brown relied on her own personal distaste for airguns in aggressively pursuing a recall of Daisy's high-velocity airguns.

In a letter announcing her resignation, dated August 8, 2001, Brown wrote:

The U.S. Consumer Product Safety Commission (CPSC) has received a great deal of attention in the last few weeks. I am very gratified by the recognition we have received for the work we do here and its importance to the American public.

There has been considerable speculation about my plans. I want to end that speculation.

President Bush is entitled to appoint his own Chairman of the CPSC. I plan to give him that opportunity. I will resign as Chairman and as a Commissioner on November 1, 2001, unless another Chairman is nominated and confirmed by the Senate before then. Nobody would be more pleased than I would if President Bush uses this opportunity to appoint a new Chairman who shares his philosophy, and also believes in the mission of this agency and will build on our work to protect the American public. I am hopeful that this announcement will provide time for another nominee to go through the confirmation process.

We have unfinished business here at the Commission. There are a number of areas where we need to take action to save children's lives before I leave. These include:

- *redesigning baby bath seats to prevent children from drowning;*

- *a major recall of (or lawsuit regarding) a very dangerous product that kills and maims children;*

- *a standard for mattresses to protect against deaths from fires;*

- *a standard for bed rails to prevent children from suffocating when their heads get entrapped between the rail and the bed; and*

- *child resistant packaging for baby oil and other similar products to prevent aspiration deaths and injuries to children.*

I plan to devote the coming months to working on these very important matters and others.

What we do at the CPSC is keep families and children safe. As you can see, I plan to continue to help doing that for the next few months. And when I leave the agency, I am going to continue working to keep families and children safe. I plan to found a non-profit foundation called SAFE - a Safer America for Everyone - that will engage business, consumers and others in this critical mission.

As long as I am Chairman, I will work with CPSC's staff to pursue our mission with all our collective energy. It is the noblest of missions. I feel privileged to have been able to work here for almost 8 years and look forward to what we will achieve in the coming months.

The second bulleted item, *a major recall of (or lawsuit regarding) a very dangerous product that kills and maims children,* indicates that Chairman Brown had already predetermined the timetable and course of a potential administrative action which had not even been put to the vote of the Commission.

The CPSC Takes Administrative Action Against Daisy

The CPSC met on Tuesday, October 23rd, and voted on the matter on October 30th, the day before out-going Chairperson Ann Brown left office. Two of the three commissioners voted to issue an administrative complaint against Daisy, seeking to force the recall of the PowerLine Model 856 and Model 880 air rifles. Daisy was served with a copy of the complaint, in Rogers, Arkansas, within minutes of the announcement in Washington, D.C..

The honorable Mary Sheila Gall, Commissioner, dissented stating,

This complaint is highly politicized, it is not well founded in law or the evidence and it should not have been brought.

In her prepared statement, Commissioner Gall pointed out several procedural irregularities in the handling of the Daisy matter:

Commission staff furnished the confidential draft Complaint to a reporter and other news organizations before the Commission voted on the issue. News organizations were also informed that the Commission would be holding a press conference at 2:00 p.m. today to announce a matter concerning a consumer product that would involve the mother of a victim.

Although the Commission staff retained both a gunsmith expert and a materials science expert to examine Daisy BB guns alleged to lodge BBs in the magazine or elsewhere, the Commission has no written report from either of these experts. Nor was the work of these experts reviewed by the Commission's own laboratory staff. When I inquired about the reason why no written report was prepared, I was told that it was part of a litigation strategy. From this I conclude that the decision was made early on to litigate this case, and the case was prepared with that objective in mind, rather than the

"...treat every gun as if it is loaded.

ordinary objective of informing the Commission as thoroughly as possible prior to a vote.

Finally, the briefing memo contains glaring errors of fact, such as a description of a BB being "chambered" into a rifle's "muzzle" and the assertion that Daisy BB guns are more "powerful" than .38 caliber revolvers.

The best explanation for these procedural irregularities can be found in Chairwoman Ann Brown's August 8, 2001 statement announcing her departure. In that statement she announced both the result of this investigation ("a lawsuit regarding a very dangerous product [which everyone at the Commission knew to be Daisy BB guns] that kills and maims children") and its timetable ("before I leave"). Yet the Commission did not receive its briefing package in the Daisy matter until October 4, 2001.

Regarding the charges of defect due to features such as gravity feed, lack of automatic safety and ease of viewing ammo in the loading port,

HIGH-POWERED AIRGUN. FOR AGES 16 YEARS OR OLDER.

⚠ **WARNING:** NOT A TOY. ADULT SUPERVISION REQUIRED. MISUSE OR CARELESS USE MAY CAUSE SERIOUS INJURY OR DEATH. MAY BE DANGEROUS UP TO 286 YARDS (261 METERS).

Commissioner Gall stated,

I find none of these theories of defect persuasive when applied to the specific Daisy designs in question, because they are industry-wide.

Daisy Defends Common Sense

Daisy responded to the allegations stating that any firearm or airgun may, at some time, fail to feed or fire. That, however, provides no excuse for irresponsible actions such as cocking, pointing and firing a gun at another human being. It was Daisy's position that adult supervision, common sense and responsible judgment combined with adequate package warnings and instructional operations manuals already prevent risk-taking behavior in the vast majority of rational young adult and adult shooters.

On the subject of automatic safeties, Daisy pointed out that almost no firearms have automatic safeties. Because airguns are used in training shooters and because many experienced firearms shooters use airguns for inexpensive marksmanship practice, airgun features do and should closely mimic those of firearms. Additionally, the company maintained, no mechanical safety device can take the place of the shooter's judgment.

While Daisy stated that BBs are easily seen in the open visible loading port, a common rule of gun safety instructs shooters to always "treat every gun as if it is loaded." The CPSC's implication was that, if the BB is difficult to see, the shooter may fire the gun at another human being. Daisy replied that, under this scenario, the defect is with the judgment or behavior of the shooter, not the airgun.

The airguns attacked by the CPSC are intended only for adults and young adults, sixteen years of age or older, with adult supervision (as the product packaging clearly denotes). At age sixteen, a young adult can obtain a driver's license in most states and be solely responsible for his or her actions in a car.

The fact that a small minority of users ignore common sense, set aside their safety training, ignore warnings, point a gun toward another human being and pull the trigger should not be the basis for liability of a manufacturer. Equating blatant product misuse or careless misuse with product defect waives all personal accountability for actions and makes a mockery of personal and parental responsibility.

Daisy stood its ground, acknowledging that its products are guns and must be treated with respect. They have no defect nor do they pose undue danger when properly used and when basic gun safety rules are adhered to. When the most basic of gun safety rules ("Keep the muzzle pointed in a safe direction" and "Always assume every gun is loaded") are ignored, or when the product is misused, carelessly, recklessly or criminally used, there are often consequences for the behavior.

The defense against this complaint would cost the company hundreds of thousands of dollars, several trips to Washington, D.C., and many sleepless nights for Daisy's management team.

Daisy retained Locker Greenberg & Brainin, P.C., a law firm seasoned in and actively engaged in the representation of many large international and national trade associations and corporations. Their expertise is the representation of associations and corporations in negotiations and proceedings before independent U.S. regulatory agencies such as the CPSC as well as the Federal Trade Commission and the U.S. Food and Drug Administration. Additionally, senior members of the firm participate in and advise many voluntary standards committees, helping to develop standards to ensure the safe use of a wide range of consumer products.

Upon invitation, Daisy briefed both Representative Stearn's staff from the Energy and Commerce Committee and Representative Greenwood's staff on the Oversight Committee on the irregularities, improprieties and politicization of this investigation.

In an effort to bring reason to the highly politicized situation, Daisy delivered a letter to President George W. Bush. The letter opened with this statement:

Daisy Outdoor Products is a historic American company that has been severely damaged by the recent actions of an administrative agency out of control, the Consumer Products Safety Commission. Our company believes that any fair and reasonable review of the investigation will uncover unreasonable and shameless abuse of process and abuse of power by this Commission. The setting aside and deliberate ignoring of over 20 years of CPSC expert review and analysis of airguns, in favor of undisclosed oral opinions of plaintiff's attorney experts, is highly subjective and contrary to the entire administrative purpose and procedure. The CPSC is designed to review and investigate products, and Daisy has never objected to being under scrutiny. This abuse has resulted in tremendous expense to Daisy and at the expense of taxpayer money. Although ignored by the CPSC, Daisy's requests have remained the same from the beginning of this investigation: fairness, reasonableness, non-politicization of issues, and due process.

The three page letter outlined substantial economic damages as well as damages to Daisy's name and reputation caused by the CPSC's abuse of power. The company's ability to secure competitively priced insurance was negatively impacted. The legal defense itself was expensive. Additionally, the company experienced a loss in productivity as thousands of hours of work were necessarily diverted from selling, marketing and management to defensive rhetoric. Daisy, long known for working with youth, civic and conservation organizations as well as the branches of the U.S. armed forces to promote the safe use of airguns was being accused of making a defective product, solely because of potential abuse and misuse. Damage to the company's reputation and goodwill was immeasurable.

In a call for remedy, the letter stated,

The merits of the case are baseless; the CPSC's own investigations have proved Daisy's products to be non-defective. The Commission has engaged in selective prosecution, breaching confidentiality, refusing to provide discovery, amid procedural irregularities of re-opening an investigation, mishandling, abuse of discretion, and refusal to seek a reasonable resolution.

In closing the letter, Ray Hobbs, Daisy's President & C.E.O. passionately implored,

Mr. President, we plead for your involvement in reversing this unwarranted administrative action. Daisy takes great pride in our rich 115-year heritage and we're anxious to get back to business as usual – growing our company and providing jobs for Americans. Thank you for your intervention and we look forward to your response.

Consent Agreement Reached

The company was never able to receive any confirmation that President Bush became involved in the action, however on November 14, 2003, Daisy reached a consent agreement with the CPSC, under the direction of Chairman Hal Stratton. Daisy agreed to launch a $1.5 million safety campaign and place additional warnings on its packaging, advising users to always treat guns as if they are loaded (warnings which were already present, in other forms, in the operations manuals).

In a nine page statement written regarding the proposed consent agreement, the honorable Mary Sheila Gall, Commissioner, stated,

The reckless abuse of a weapon is simply not a risk against which this Commission can reasonably ask manufacturers to guard. This type of risk is inherent in the nature of the instrument. The Commission must rely on individual and parental responsibility in limiting the adverse consequences of BB gun use. One of the most important decisions that a parent will ever make is when to entrust a young person with a BB gun or a firearm without supervision, and one of the most consequential decisions any individual can make is to pull a trigger on (a) BB gun or firearm. When tragedies happen with reasonably safe products such as the Model 856 and 880 air rifles, they result from the irresponsibility of the user, or poor parental and caregiver judgment, not the inherent nature of the instrument.

In closing, Commissioner Gall stated,

The record shows that this is a case that should not have been brought in the first place, and which has now been settled on terms substantially similar to those that Daisy proposed over fourteen months ago. Students of government who wish to see how the regulatory enforcement process can be used to harass a small company to no good purpose need look no further than this action for a splendid case study. I hope that in the future, the Commission will take much greater care in deciding which actions to bring, and exercise greater oversight of pending actions, in its effort to protect the public from genuine product hazards.

In 2003, on the occasion of the consent agreement, CPSC Chairman Hal Stratton wrote in his statement,

Prior to the investigation that led to the filing of this case, the Commission investigated air guns seven separate times, utilizing a variety of disciplines, including engineering and human factors. With the exception of the investigation leading to this case, none of the investigations resulted in a preliminary determination that the product represented a substantial product hazard. In addition, these investigations showed that the air guns met existing voluntary standards. The Commission has never found that air rifles or any model of air rifle, constitute a substantial product hazard.

In his Analysis of Facts, Chairman Stratton concluded,

> "...The record shows that this is a case that should not have been brought in the first place, and which has now been settled on terms substantially similar to those that Daisy proposed over fourteen months ago. Students of government who wish to see how the regulatory enforcement process can be used to harass a small company to no good purpose need look no further than this action for a splendid case study.
>
> – Mary Sheila Gall, Commissioner

All of the injuries that can be attributed to the guns at issue in this case were preventable. They all involved either someone pointing the gun at someone and pulling the trigger or playing with the gun in an inappropriate manner – all in violation of widely known and accepted safety rules for the use of guns.

Two Years and Fifteen Days

October 30, 2001, to November 14, 2003. For two years and fifteen days the future of Daisy and even the future of airguns as a product category had been threatened for no more valid reason than that the product could be irresponsibly misused.

Chapter 10

A Museum With a History

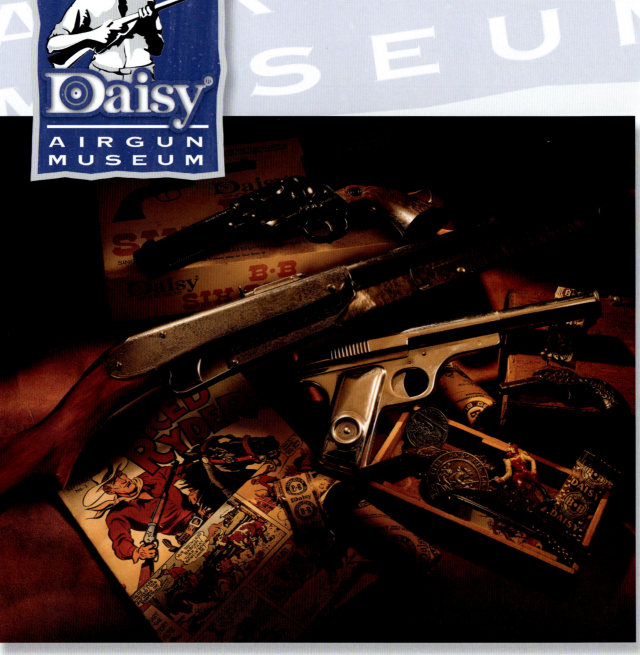

Museums are established to collect historical data and artifacts, to preserve them and to make them available for enjoyment and research. It's hard to believe, therefore, that a museum could create a history of its own.

How fortunate it is for Daisy's current management team that their predecessors placed value on preserving the company's past. The Daisy Museum inherited an amazing collection of airguns dating to the 17th century, as well as excellent examples of most every model of Daisy ever made.

Collecting Artifacts

Where did all of these guns come from and how were they earmarked for posterity? In recent years it has been the company's policy to archive two samples of every new model. Daisy's customer service department often would set aside a small inventory of each model to be used for parts and repairs.

In the 1920s Cass Hough had discovered a cache of old Daisy guns in Fred Lefever's office. He identified and tagged them with the intention of, someday, having a Daisy Museum. One of the largest single sources of older guns for the museum was a trade-in promotion implemented in the years of the Great Depression. A customer could send their old Daisy to the company and pay the difference in value to receive a new Daisy. An estimated

DO LIKE YOUR DAD AND MOTHER DO
Your dad trades his old car in on a new one—your mother trades her old vacuum cleaner or washing machine for the latest models. If your present air rifle isn't all it should be—if it doesn't shoot every shot hard and true, write and tell us how old it is, and what condition it's in, and we'll make you a proposition you'll like—to trade it in on a brand new, 1933 model Daisy of your own choosing. Write us NOW, and you'll have our proposition by return mail.

100,000 guns were dug out of closets, trunks, garages, sheds and attics and mailed to Daisy. Of course, the primary goal of the promotion was not to increase sales directly to the consumer. Rather, it was to place new product in the marketplace, to re-stimulate interest in the category and to help move inventory from the shelves of the company's retail customers.

Some of the guns from the trade-in promotion were added to the inventory of guns tagged by Cass. Just before the start of World War II, the lobby of the office at the plant in Plymouth, Michigan, was remodeled and a display case was built along one wall. It was there that Hough would store the old guns he had tagged. While he dreamed of a museum of antique Daisy guns, it would not be built until well after the company relocated to Rogers, Arkansas.

Courtesy of the Plymouth Historical Museum, Plymouth, MI

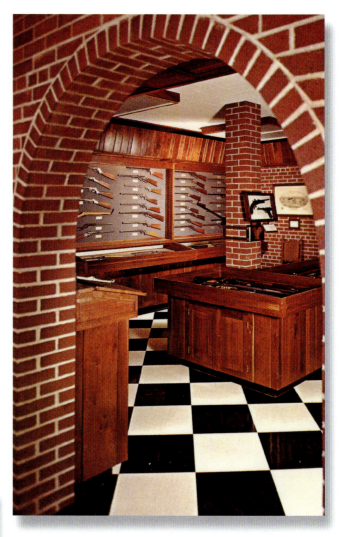

Establishing the Daisy Museum

Eight years following the relocation to Rogers, Arkansas, in 1958, a small brick room with black and white floor tiles was added to the northwest corner of the Daisy offices on Eighth Street in Rogers. In the room were six upright cases and two floor display cases, designed and built by retired Army Colonel and local artisan Edward A. Rew of Rogers, Arkansas, from native black walnut. The wood for the cases was air dried and finished in Rogers. On September 21, 1966, the International Daisy Airgun Museum was completed and dedicated to Charley Bennett and Edward Hough.

Up until November 1999 Daisy still occupied the office building at 2111 South Eighth Street; however, only BBs were being produced in the adjacent plant. The small museum room was just off the reception area. There was no chronological organization to the presentation of the old Daisy airguns, little descriptive information and there was no gift shop. Essentially, it was a self-guided tour of eight cases filled with BB guns.

The plant and offices were on the real estate market at that time. When the plant was sold in July 1999 the purchasers of the property gave Daisy until Thanksgiving weekend to re-locate. A building was available in an industrial park in the north part of Rogers and offices were built to accommodate Daisy's staff.

The museum, however, if it was ever to become a tourist attraction, would not thrive in the industrial park setting. Rogers was still in a building boom. Real estate was scarce and rent factors were high. Joe Murfin consulted with the city's new mayor, Steve Womack, about Daisy's desire to have the museum become a tourist attraction for the City. Mayor Womack was a Daisy fan and a tremendous help in finding an old 1906 bank building downtown at 114 South First Street which would serve as the first home for the Rogers Daisy Airgun Museum.

The bank building was owned by architects Perry Butcher and John Mack. Coincidentally, it was Perry Butcher who had been the architect on the museum room at the Eighth Street plant. In 2000, when the old worn burlap in the backs of all of the display cases was replaced, it was

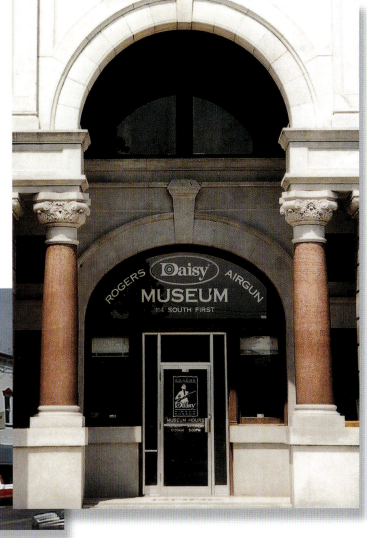

discovered that what was thought to be beige burlap had actually once been blue. Lighting in the cases had bleached out the color, leaving blue silhouettes where guns had hung. Perry had specified that fabric thirty-four years earlier and requested a piece of the faded fabric. It was not until the Daisy Museum was opened that it was discovered that the building had once housed the Rogers Historical Museum.

To prepare for the relocation of the collection, each gun was tagged and boxed individually. The ends of the boxes were labeled and the boxes were secured in locked wooden crates. The collection remained in storage from July 1999 until March 2000. Taylor Displays, a local display company, stored not only those crates but also many file cabinets and storage boxes of paper artifacts which had been sorted by decade.

The vertical walnut cases themselves had problems. Having stood against the exterior brick walls of the old museum room, they had drawn moisture and were infested with termites. While it would have been less expensive to create new cases, the old walnut cases were fumigated. End and back panels were removed and replaced with laminate covered medium density fiberboard while the walnut facades were retained.

The historic bank building on First Street had a history of its own. It had a beautiful mosaic tile floor that was white with accents of rust and dark green. In the center there was an oval area floored in wood that was directly under what used to be an oval opening in the ceiling. This area was where the teller cage was once located. There was an outside entrance to a staircase that led upstairs. In the early days of this bank building, merchants would climb the stairs after banking hours, lean out over the oval opening and drop their deposit bag into the teller cage below. This bank building was also the first in Rogers to include both a men's and women's restroom. Because men, in this era, typically

handled household and business finances, other banks did not offer a women's restroom.

While the museum staff valued the local history and truly loved the ambiance of the old bank building, it did present limitations. Rightfully so, the owners forbade the Daisy Museum, as a tenant, to anchor anything to the mosaic tile floor and permitted only limited access to hang displays on the walls. As historians, the Daisy Museum staff respected their wishes, although the owners' restrictions did challenge the museum staff to build the displays that were needed.

As a result, a free-standing museum display wall was purchased and used to create a hallway along the south wall of the museum. A clear Plexiglas window, with concentric target rings, was set into the wall, teasing visitors to look ahead at additional gun displays. Down the length of the temporary wall ran a detailed historic timeline.

Select posters, ads, photos and letters were chosen for six Plexiglas display panels, each of which represented two decades of history. These were hung on the south wall, on a mounting rail to minimize damage to the old plastered brick wall. As visitors walked down the hallway, they could read the timeline on the right and be treated to old ads, letters, photos and comics – from the 1880s to present day – in these Plexiglas display panels.

As visitors reached the end of the hallway at the back of the museum, they found themselves in a single large room with the old walnut cases

lining the wall and sitting in the middle of the room. The backside of the free-standing museum display wall featured information about airgun spring, pneumatic and CO_2 power systems, how BBs are made and some large graphics of current packaging. Like any museum worth its salt, the exit was through the gift shop.

A Unique Partnership
Because Daisy had never dedicated personnel to giving museum tours and because a new free-standing museum would require several people to staff, Joe Murfin approached Mayor Womack about asking the director of the Rogers Historical Museum to absorb the responsibilities of this new downtown museum. The Rogers Historical Museum could not manage a private collection because of stipulations in current and potential grants.

The City of Rogers Parks and Recreation director, Jim Welch, however, was excited at the opportunity to get involved and volunteered to establish the Daisy Airgun Museum as a City of Rogers Park. Frankly, he was the right man for the right job at the right time. With the help of Mayor Womack, a unique partnership with the City of Rogers was created. The City of Rogers provided staffing and managed the day-to-day operation of the museum. Geneva Guyll welcomed visitors at the front reception desk, where donations were accepted. In addition, Daisy retirees David Gates and John Ford were retained to give tours at the museum.

Daisy maintained ownership of the collection. Landlords Perry Butcher and John Mack presented the museum with a lease at a rate substantially below the market average. While there was no admission fee, donations were accepted. Gift shop sales were limited to Daisy's existing product line and sales were minimal. At the end of each year, the City of Rogers would present Daisy with a statement of earnings that always featured red ink. Daisy would then present a check to the City of Rogers that was equal to that deficit.

Being managed by the City provided access to the Parks Deptartment staff that could, cost-efficiently, do the type of odd jobs that arise when establishing and running a museum. Jim Welch had a great team including Stan Weaver, Doyle Bradford, Kenny Eaton, Dicky Paris and others who could build display cases, change light bulbs and repair plumbing - just like they would at any other Parks facility. Jim loved the museum, had a good knowledge of Daisy and took a lot of personal pride in his management of the museum.

Grand Opening Ribbon Shooting

The occasion of the museum's grand opening purposely coincided with a tour of downtown Rogers by then Arkansas First Lady Janet Huckabee, arranged by Main Street Rogers. Adam Blalock, Daisy's President & C.E. O., and Joe Murfin drove to Springdale to board an Arkansas & Missouri Railroad coach along with other community leaders and Mrs. Huckabee's entourage. When the train arrived in Rogers the rainy weather had cleared and everyone walked across First Street to the Daisy Museum.

On the steps outside the front door was a pellet trap, sitting on bales of hay. In front of the target trap was a balloon with a ribbon tied to both ends. A target was taped to the balloon. When First Lady Huckabee aimed the Daisy Mossy Oak Grizzly Model 840C and shot the target with a pellet, the balloon burst and the ribbon dropped. This may have been the first and only ribbon shooting ceremony at the grand opening of a Rogers business.

Mrs. Huckabee also visited the airgun range set up in the basement of the museum and shot a second gun to christen the range. She autographed both of those guns, one of which remains in the museum's archives and the second of which was purchased in a silent auction on the occasion of Daisy's Homecoming, Fifty Years in Rogers celebration in 2008.

Friends of the Daisy Museum

Daisy retirees with an interest in preserving the collection and supporting the efforts of the museum created a non-profit corporation entitled Friends of the Daisy Airgun Museum. Through this non-profit, they had the ability to solicit donations of cash and artifacts. Over the course of three years, the "Friends" collected $4,750 in donations which would eventually be dedicated to the restoration of the old Daisy sign and another $6,000 in additional unrestricted donations.

Protecting The Rogers Daisy Airgun Museum

Long term, however, it was neither Daisy's nor the City's intention to operate the Museum jointly. From 2000 to 2003 Daisy had continued to subsidize the museum annually so that it would not be a burden on the taxpayers. In 2003 Daisy President & C.E.O. Ray Hobbs began studying the question of whether it was more prudent to continue to subsidize the Museum or to create a separate non-profit corporation to own and manage it. With his guidance, on January 1, 2004, a business plan for the Museum was drafted that included the creation of a new non-profit corporation.

The non-profit corporation ensures that, regardless of Daisy's future ownership or existence, this amazing collection of airguns and artifacts can remain in the City of Rogers for the benefit of the City and the enjoyment of Daisy retirees, Rogers citizens and tourists.

Charter members of the board of the non-profit included Joe Murfin as chairman, Ray Hobbs and Marianne McBeth. Marianne was Daisy's in-house corporate attorney at the time and she was instrumental in the establishment of the museum as a separate non-profit corporation. In June 2004, upon the dissolution of the Friends of the Daisy Museum, the board created two new positions and elected Orin Ribar and David Gates.

Location, Location, Location

While the museum was content with its First Street location, in 2004 board member Ray Hobbs made a proposal to the Board of Directors. Ray's company, D & R Hobbs Properties, LLC, owned a historic building on the southwest corner of Second and Walnut Streets. The D&R Hobbs building dates to 1896, was once Ford's Grocery, and is known to many residents as the former Rexall Drug building. While maintaining offices upstairs, D&R Hobbs had always leased the downstairs prime retail space to specialty retail merchants. Ray was interested in having the Daisy Museum as a long-term tenant and made the board an offer which it could not refuse.

On October 25, 2004, the Museum was relocated to the D&R Hobbs Building. The new location, still home to the Daisy Museum today, offered downtown Rogers' highest traffic count comprised of residents and tourists, visiting historic downtown Rogers and passing through town on their way to Beaver Lake, Pea Ridge National Military Park, Eureka Springs and Branson. D & R Hobbs Properties allowed the museum to build interior walls to further define periods in Daisy's history. In conjunction with the Museum relocation, the staff hosted a relocation celebration and open house on Sunday, November 14th, with a ribbon cutting and silent auction.

John Ford was appointed to fill David Gate's term on the Board of Directors when David passed away in 2005. When Marianne McBeth left the company, Daisy retiree Jim Sawyer joined the board.

There are thousands of Daisy collectors, many of whom send photos of their impressive collections to the Daisy Museum. Some specialize in a single Daisy model. Others collect BB packages, catalogs, promotional literature, photos and newsletters. They search internet auctions, exchange information on "Daisy Talk" on the Museum's website, attend airgun shows, auctions and estate sales and scour antique shops, flea markets and pawn shops in order to expand their collections.

Limited Edition Collectibles

In the 1990s Daisy had been successful in marketing limited edition collectible Daisy BB guns directly to the collector market. The Gold Rush, American Boy, Pony Express, Christmas Morning, Roy Rogers and Dale Evans, Roy Rogers and Trigger and Roy Rogers and Gabby Hayes guns were serially numbered and came with a certificate of authenticity.

When the Daisy Museum established its gift shop, it took over the function of creating and marketing these limited edition guns and issued a Roy and Dusty gun, the fourth Roy Rogers gun in the series.

Today, the Friends of the Daisy Museum number over 750. Friends pay a fifty dollar lifetime membership in order to support the museum and receive a membership number, ranging from 003 up to the total number of Friends. Each time the museum issues a limited edition collectible airgun, the guns are serially numbered. The Museum retains guns number one and two then each Friend has first right to purchase his Friends' numbered gun. Because not every Friend exercises his right to purchase his numbered gun, even some low numbered collectible guns will be offered in the gift shop and via the website to the general public. The museum's Friends volunteer and assist the museum in many ways. Some help to publicize the museum and its new products to fellow collectors through email newsletters and magazine articles. The museum depends on other knowledgeable collectors to provide research or to validate historical information. When the museum needed to invest several thousands of dollars in hardware and technology to implement a comprehensive audio tour, the Friends contributed money which totally underwrote that cost. Truly, when the group was established, the correct title was chosen: Friends.

Preserving While Growing and Changing

The Daisy Museum's amazing collection of artifacts includes airguns from the 17th and 18th centuries as well as most every Daisy gun ever made. It is complemented by a wonderful display of ads, packaging, calendars, clocks, signs, paintings, letters and promotional materials. While the collection is growing slowly, thanks to generous donations from collectors and retirees, the museum staff is making constant improvements and additions to the displays and the Rogers Daisy Airgun Museum continues to evolve.

By continually improving displays and expanding the experience of touring the museum, the Daisy Museum promotes the amazing history of the Daisy company. Additionally the museum serves a local community of Daisy staff, retirees and general public, all of whom take pride in bringing friends, business associates and visiting relatives to the museum. The museum proudly and gratefully serves the City of Rogers, the Northwest Arkansas Region and the State of Arkansas by providing a unique destination which draws tourists from all over the country. And, the museum is diligent to serve our Friends and the entire community of Daisy collectors who anxiously await the next limited edition Daisy.

Chapter 11

Are We Home Yet?

One of the largest and most significant undertakings by the Friends of the Daisy Museum was the total restoration of the antique Daisy neon sign which was originally erected in 1960 in front of the company's manufacturing facility on South Eighth Street.

The sign, measuring 24' wide by 16' high, featured blinking lights, simulating action of a BB streaming across the sign, followed by a progression of neon letters lighting. When the last BB bulb, closest to the center target in the letter D was lit, the neon ring of the target lit, followed by individual letters: D – A – I – S – Y. Once all letters were lit, the sign went dark only to start the procedure of streaming BB lights all over again.

No doubt, in 1960 the sign was ahead of its time. Had the original concept been developed as submitted by the sign manufacturer, there would have been a sign in the shape of a shooter with an airgun, shooting an arc of BBs (lights on arched wires) over Eighth Street to connect with the rectangular sign. Even in those days city leaders obviously felt that such a sign would pose an unsafe distraction for drivers.

Today, the City of Rogers has grown south on Eighth Street, or Highway 71, beyond where the original Daisy plant used to be. However, in 1960 the Daisy plant marked the southern reaches of the city. Daisy retirees and long-time residents would tell you that they knew they had arrived in Rogers when they saw the Daisy neon sign.

In 1999 when Daisy sold the Eighth Street property and moved the corporate offices to an industrial park on Stribling Drive, off of Second Street on the north side of Rogers, the sign had not been operational for several years. It was taken down, dismantled and put in storage.

Nabholtz Construction Company donated the use of a crane and flatbed semi-trailer. The City of Rogers Parks Department employees positioned web straps around the sign. The crane supported the weight of each sign panel as a Parks Department employee climbed between the two panels and used a torch to cut the sign's angle-iron frame from the vertical I-beam posts. Once each sign panel was free, the crane set it on the semi flatbed to be transported to storage on Nabholtz property. The sign would be later moved to the Parks Department maintenance facility, where each panel was dismantled and the lettering removed.

The sign had suffered years of neglect and was in sad condition. In 2001 the non-profit Daisy Airgun Museum undertook a lengthy fundraising campaign to restore the sign to its original condition, replacing all of the electrical elements, missing and damaged parts, filling holes, sanding and repainting it to its original dark blue color and mounting the two faces on a new three-post structure. On several occasions it became obvious that a new sign could have been built for less money than it cost to restore the vintage sign.

At a critical point in the restoration process, Ken Jones, Sr. of Ken's Signs contacted the company to determine the lighting sequence for the incandescent bulbs and neon tubing on the sign. The company polled a

dozen Daisy retirees, asked their opinions and got as many different versions. Fortunately, the name of the company which had made the electronics for the old sign was marked inside one of the panels. When contacted, they had the original order for the sequence and were able to supply a new electronic box.

The City of Rogers granted a variance for the off premises sign to be relocated at the north entryway to Historic Downtown Rogers, classifying it as an antique instead of a billboard sign.

Ken's Signs completed the restoration at a cost of $16,284 and re-erected the sign on May 9, 2007. On May 14th, under a tent in front of the Daisy plant at the corner of Second Street and Stribling Drive, a dedication ceremony was held. The Mayor of Rogers, Steve Womack and Daisy's President & C.E.O., Ray Hobbs, threw the switch on the breaker box to officially re-light the old sign.

The Daisy Airgun Museum underwrote $4,584 of the cost of the project. $11,700 was donated by local citizens and Daisy collectors who support the non-profit Daisy Airgun Museum. The cost of the entire project was reduced by generous in-kind donations. Southwest Power and Electric, Rodden Landscaping, Rescue Heroes and Crossland Construction, BEI Electric, Rogers Iron and Metal, D & R Hobbs Properties and Ken's Signs were all generous with their support,

time, professional expertise and materials.

Although now on the north side of town, the restored antique Daisy neon sign once again announces to our visitors that they have arrived in Rogers and to Rogers' residents that they are home.

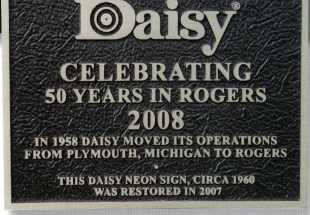

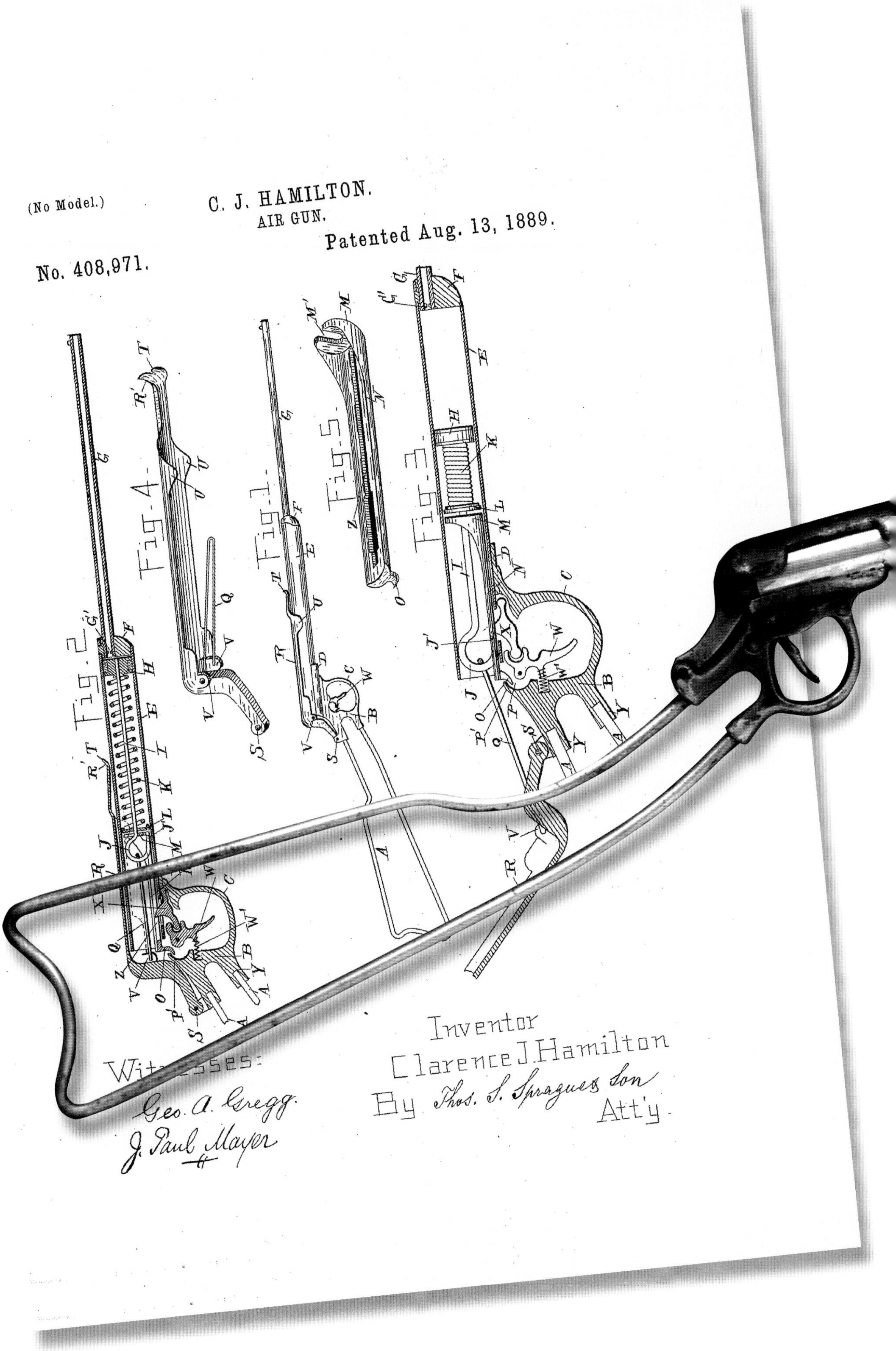

(No Model.)
C. J. HAMILTON.
AIR GUN.
Patented Aug. 13, 1889.
No. 408,971.
Fig. 1.
Fig. 2.
Fig. 3.
Fig. 4.
Fig. 5.
Inventor
Clarence J. Hamilton
By Thos. S. Sprague & Son
Att'y.
Witnesses:
Geo. A. Gregg.
J. Paul Mayer

CHAPTER 12
ONCE EVERY 120 YEARS

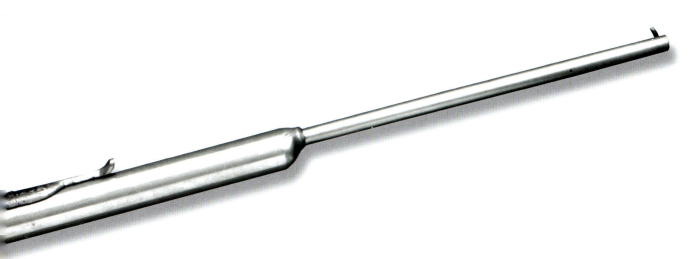

There is a saying at Daisy: It All Starts Here. With a Daisy.

Certainly for most people, their first gun is a Daisy BB gun. And for Daisy, it all started with Clarence Hamilton's little wire frame gun, commonly referred to as a wirestock BB gun. Oddly enough, while the Daisy Museum owns several first models in different variations, it does not have a pre-patent model in its collection. This variation is distinguished by the lack of a brace where the stock enters the cast trigger guard halves.

The first Daisy airgun was, technically, not made by Daisy but by the Plymouth Iron Windmill Company of Plymouth, Michigan. An invention of Clarence Hamilton, the little top-cocking steel gun was brought to Plymouth Iron Windmill Company because they had the tooling and capability to produce it. The windmill company's general manager shot the prototype gun and exclaimed, "Boy, that's a Daisy."

The first guns, made in 1888 before a patent was secured, were marked DAISY MFD. BY IRON WINDMILL CO. PLYMOUTH MICH PAT. APD. FOR. Daisy was then simply the name of the model of the gun. The company would not change its name to Daisy Manufacturing until 1895.

To the best of the company's knowledge, a working replica of this first airgun – the one that started it all for Daisy – had never been made.

When the Daisy Outdoor Products team decided to undertake this project, they wanted the gun to closely replicate the original. Using original patent drawings and taking measurements of parts from antique guns on loan from collectors, the team began to develop specifications and tolerances for each part.

Twenty-one Parts
There are, in fact, twenty-one parts to this gun:
- A steel wire stock
- A brass pump tube
- A brass barrel with an inside diameter of .180
- A bronze cocking lever which also serves as the rear sight
- A bronze abutment
- Two bronze trigger housing halves
  The castings for the original gun were iron and were bronzed before being plated with nickel. On this replica, they were sand-cast in bronze.
- A wire plunger rod
- A machined steel plunger
- A cocking link wire
- A machine-turned compression spring. (The original springs were hand turned.)
- Two steel machined pins to hold the two trigger housing halves together
- A pin to connect the lever to the trigger housing
- A trigger, cut from steel using CNC equipment
- A sear, cut from steel using CNC equipment
- A zinc-plated steel trigger spring
- Twenty-eight inches of candle wicking which is saturated in bee's wax then wrapped around the plunger
- A turned brass breech plug which aligns the barrel with the pump tube. (On the original gun, this piece consisted of cast lead.)
- A steel front sight
- And, there is one piece which was not on the original gun: an internal magnet which retains a steel BB when it is loaded. The original gun fired lead shot and the barrel was slightly tapered to retain the lead ball.

With the exception of the magnet, all parts for this gun were made in U.S.A. and the gun was hand-assembled in Rogers, Arkansas, at a dedicated off-site facility.

Hand Built; One at a Time
What the team learned in the process of building 1,000 of these replica guns is that, in essence, these old guns were each hand-made. With the exception of the substitution of turned brass for poured lead and the use of modern Computerized Numerical Control (CNC) equipment, the processes utilized to authentically replicate this gun were much the same in 2009 as they were in 1888.

The wire stock, the cocking link wire and the plunger rod were hand-formed using a bench jig. The plunger head was then braized to the rod.

Using a jig to ensure proper alignment, the barrel was inserted into the brass breech plug which was then inserted into the pump tube. These parts were then silver soldered together.

The front sight was inserted and braized in place.

The two trigger housing halves were received from the caster and were milled in a CNC machine to assure exact fit. The halves were pinned and braized together and excess weld slag was removed by hand grinding. The trigger and sear were then seated in the trigger housing and the two halves pinned together. The trigger housing assembly was then braized to the pump tube.

The cocking lever was received from the caster and alignment holes for the pivot pin and cocking link wire were pre-drilled. Then the cocking lever could be pinned to the trigger housing assembly.

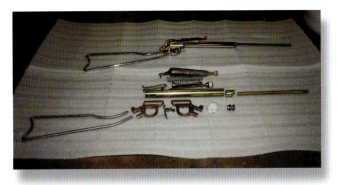

This assembly was then sandblasted. The wire stock was inserted into the trigger housing assembly and braized; then this joint was sandblasted. It was critical to have a smooth, highly-polished finish to the gun before it was nickel plated.

These limited edition airguns were serially numbered, 0001 of 1000 to 1000 of 1000 and that unique number was hand stamped into the underside of the barrel.

At this time the gun was meticulously quality checked for fit and finish then sent to the plater for nickel plating.

When returned to the assembly facility, the trigger spring was inserted. Because the spring was zinc plated, it could not be installed in the gun before it was nickel plated.

Candle wicking was tightly wound around the plunger head then soaked in bee's wax to create an airtight seal in the pump tube. The pump tube was lubricated before the plunger assembly, with spring, was inserted into the pump tube.

The cocking link wire was attached to the rear of

the plunger rod and the abutment then inserted behind the plunger assembly. The ends of the cocking link wire were then inserted into the two holes in the cocking lever.

At this point, the gun was ready for test firing and final inspection.

Attention to Detail
It's impossible to know how the first gun was packaged for shipment. An antique ad described it as being in a neat paper box. The team surmised neat to mean unadorned or plain, and used a plain Kraft package with a simple one-color label glued to the front panel. The old ad also mentioned that sample shot and a target were included so these were also included with this fully-functional replica. To minimize initial marring of the plating, a card was inserted where the cocking lever touches the pump tube.

In the tradition of other limited edition collectible airguns marketed by Daisy and the Rogers Daisy Airgun Museum, a certificate of authenticity was also included. As a bonus, collectors also received a medallion with the likeness of this replica.

To be able to make a product for over 120 years is rare. To be able to re-make a product so true to the original, after 120 years of industry innovation, is even more rare.

For the hunting and shooting sports market, it all starts with a Daisy airgun. And, for Daisy, this gun was where it all started.

Chapter 13

Thinking Outside the Daisy Box

Extending the Daisy Brand

Research has proven that the Daisy brand would, in the minds of consumers, easily transfer to outdoor sports and recreational activities other than the shooting sports. Extending the Daisy brand would provide the company with additional sales opportunities in other related outdoor sports and recreation categories. Applying the Daisy brand name to products in additional product categories would bring instant recognition and perception of value to those products by leveraging the Daisy brand equity. The additional placement of Daisy branded products would capitalize on brand loyalty and deliver added impressions for the Daisy brand.

For these reasons, extending the Daisy brand, whether through new product development or acquisition, has always been, and remains, a serious consideration. In fact, this belief was the driving force behind creating and filing the fictitious name, or doing business as (dba), Daisy Outdoor Products in 2000. Having established the corporate umbrella, Daisy is, today, still poised to capitalize on an acquisition or a line extension which would complement the brand and cost-efficiently integrate with the company's market delivery system and business model.

In the book *It's a Daisy!* Cass Hough recalls Daisy dabbling in ventures including the ZigZag Razor Strop in 1913. Daisy retirees tell of an infrared target system and a motion detector security system being made by Daisy. In other words, as with most things at Daisy, what current management has discovered is that creating a line extension or leveraging the Daisy brand is a concept that has been under consideration for a good number of the company's 125 years.

Sta Dri Boots

Following the passing of Charles Bennett in 1956 and the passing of E.C. Hough in 1959, the company sold, in 1960, to Murchison Brothers, an insurance and investment company. Murchison Brothers of Dallas, Texas, owned Heddon Fishing Tackle as well as the Ranger Boot and Shoe Company of Kileen, Texas, makers of the Sta Dri Boot. The Sta Dri boot was an excellent, waterproof outdoor boot, although very expensive. Murchison challenged Daisy with the development of Heddon and Sta Dri sales. Daisy was unable to place the boots with any major shoe store chain (as most of them were affiliated with shoe manufacturers) and could not generate adequate sales volume through sporting goods outlets. While a superior product, lack of placement forced the company to liquidate the inventory in 1963.

Toy Trucks

In 1963 Daisy sourced a line of battery operated toys, under the Daisymatic brand. However, the company quickly discovered that, to stay in the toy business, they would need to expand the line. After careful consideration, Daisy decided to concentrate on airguns and get out of the toy truck business.

When Victor Comptometer acquired Daisy from the Murchison Brothers, they were in the process of diversification through building a recreation products group including several companies whose products fell into the lifetime sports category. While under common ownership of Victor Comptometer, Ertl and Daisy cooperated on the sales of Daisy toy guns and Ertl die cast farm toys. Up to that point, Ertl had marketed its farm toys through farm equipment dealers and didn't have a sales force experienced in calling on retail buyers. Daisy's sales force included two separate teams. One called on sporting goods buyers and sold airguns, while another team called on toy buyers and sold toy guns. Daisy turned over its toy office at 200 Fifth Avenue in New York City to Ertl. The Ertl management team absorbed the Daisy toy sales force in order to represent both toy guns and die cast toys.

Contract Manufacturing

In Rogers, Arkansas, in the 1960s through 1990s, Daisy operated a modern, vertically integrated manufacturing operation in a facility occupying more than 325,000 square feet. About the only parts Daisy didn't manufacture during the 1940s through the 1980s were springs, nuts, bolts and molded rubber parts. Upon the relocation to Rogers in 1958 the company didn't move its wood shaping equipment and began to purchase wood stocks, at first with Moser Furniture Company of Rogers.

Capabilities included precision punch press

operation, extruding, zinc and aluminum die-casting, tool-making, CNC machining, injection molding, silk-screening, painting and finishing operations. An existing work force was skilled at production, assembly and packaging. The capabilities of both the plant and the workforce had a nationwide reputation for meeting rigid quality control standards. These capabilities, coupled with seasonality of its own products, allowed Daisy to market these services and contract manufacture for other companies. Daisy marketed these capabilities under a division called Daisy Contract Manufacturing Service. There were a variety of products manufactured under contract including barbeque utensils and die-cast fan blade brackets for Hunter ceiling fans. Stair-stepper exercise equipment, promoted via television advertorials ("as seen on TV"), were assembled at Daisy.

Caseless Firearms and Ammunition

In 1961, using a traditional break barrel pellet rifle, Jules Van Langenhoven, a chemical engineer from Belgium, and J.J. Guardiola Aragones demonstrated a caseless ammunition firearm concept for Cass Hough. Hough was impressed by the demonstration which involved placing a small pinch of cotton-like material behind the pellet prior to firing.

The cotton wadding system, however, was impractical because it was impossible to regulate the amount used. Van Langenhoven moved his family to Rogers, Arkansas, to work with Dick Daniel and Ron Joyce of Daisy's Research and Development department to help formulate the propellant and finalize a gun and ammunition which Daisy could market. Daisy's VL gun, the first successful, commercially-offered firearm which did not utilize a brass casing, primer and gunpowder, was named after the inventor Van Langenhoven.

It was in the Daisy office cafeteria that Dick Daniel first combined Nitric Acid and Sulfuric Acid in order to nitrate cotton, essentially duplicating the material Van Langenhoven had originally used. Dick consulted with the Illinois Institute of Technology Research Institute in Chicago to finalize the ultimate formulation of salt granulation which would create the necessary porosity of the propellant.

In developing the final nitrocellulose propellant, a compounded salt was mixed with the nitrocellulose. When a solvent was added, it yielded a plastic-like material which could be injected onto the base of a lead bullet. The material was then bathed in yet another solvent which did not attack the nitrocellulose but did leach out the salt. The result was a porous nitrocellulose material with many small fissures filled with needle-like projections which would enable the material to be ignited by compressed air.

The gun itself featured a piston which compressed air in a cylinder. A jet of air, heated to 2000° F, was forced through a ball check valve into the chamber where it ignited the propellant which was fused to a .22 caliber, 29 grain solid lead bullet.

From start to finish, the project spent seven years in development. The first guns were produced November 13, 1967, and offered for sale on May 13, 1968. The market for firearms was diminished in 1968 following the assassinations of President John F. Kennedy and Martin Luther King. Only 25,000 of the guns were made.

Firearms

Because a Daisy is traditionally a shooter's first BB gun, the company theorized that a Daisy .22 caliber rifle could easily capture a market position as a shooter's first firearm. With an

interest in extending the Daisy brand from airguns to firearms, Daisy began to develop one entry level price point rifle.

In 1987 Jerry Haskins and Earl Reddick, local gunsmiths, were building firearms for the Navy Seals. Reddick was employed by Daisy and Haskins was retained as a consultant to work on the prospect of Daisy entering the firearms arena. Daisy used its Research and Development department, housed in a free standing building on the plant's property, to assemble those bolt-action, single-shot .50 caliber rifles as well as the NATO .762 caliber rifle.

Don Fleming was a model maker for Daisy and worked with Haskins and Reddick. Daisy marketed the guns to The Crane Division (NSWC Crane), one of the Naval Surface Warfare Centers in Crane, Indiana.

These rifles had fluted barrels and muzzle brakes and came with a bipod. The guns were all black and featured a composite frame stock. None of the guns produced for the Navy Seals were marked as a Daisy product. In the U.S. Army's Aberdine Proving Ground, Aberdine, Maryland, Daisy employee John Ford witnessed the .50 cal. rifle successfully hitting an exploding target with a tracer round at 1500 meters, just short of one mile.

As a result of this research and development and firearms manufacturing experience, and already holding a Bureau of Alcohol, Tobacco, Firearms and Explosives-issued license to manufacture firearms, Daisy was prepared to venture into the development of an entry price point .22 caliber rifle for the consumer market. Daisy's Legacy line of rim fire rifles, chambered in .22 Long Rifle, were made from 1989 to 1991. The line included three models: a single shot, bolt-action model 2201 with plastic stock and forearm /2211 with wood stock and forearm; a ten-shot, bolt action, rotary clip repeater, models 2202/2212; and a semi-automatic repeater with a seven-shot in-line clip, models 2203/2213. Each had an octagonal barrel shroud. Models with plastic stocks featured an adjustable butt plate.

Adding attractive features may have added value but it also increased the price to the point that, while the Daisy Legacy was competitive with other leading .22s, it was not the entry price point in the category.

Daisy's experience with the Legacy line did enable the company to do a favor for a major retail customer. Wal-Mart had purchased a black, composite stock .22 caliber rifle from Iver Johnson of Jacksonville, Arkansas. When Iver Johnson was unable to complete an order in November 1986, Wal-Mart approached Daisy and requested that the company purchase the remaining inventory of parts from Iver Johnson and finish the assembly of the guns to fulfill Wal-Mart's outstanding orders.

Quickpitch Tents, by Daisy
In 1989, inspired by tents used by utility companies to protect workers and equipment in inclement weather, Daisy marketed a line of tents for the recreational camping market, under the Quickpitch sub-brand. The tent line

included a two-person 5'X 8' tent, a four-person 8.5' X 8' and a six person 11'X 12' tent. Bob Reid and Buddy Pilgrim of Daisy collaborated with the T.A. Pelsue Company, known for its integral frame tents for industrial, military and commercial use, for the production of these tents. Mark Erickson, co-inventor of the first geodesic dome tent, was consulted on the design. The tents featured a patented hub and strut exoskeleton construction with a skin of lightweight Nylon Taffeta and a breathable canopy. The walls, floors and zippers were urethane-coated for rain protection. Doors and windows featured No-See-Um mesh for ventilation. The company boldly claimed that a Quickpitch tent could be set up in less than thirty seconds.

Paintball Markers

While Daisy never marketed a paintball marker under the Daisy brand, the company was involved in the early development of paintball markers. The Nelson Paint Company introduced paintballs in the 1960s as a method of marking trees. Different colors of paint were being brushed on logs to segregate logs according to which mill they were to be shipped. Nelson's gelatin capsule, injected with paint and fired

from a modified CO_2 pistol, represented a superior method by which to mark the logs from some distance. Crosman first manufactured markers for Nelson, which marketed them as the Nel-Spot 707.

The first marker specifically to be used with paintballs was designed by Daisy engineer James Hale in 1970 and named the Splotchmarker. Under an agreement with Nelson Paint Company, the Splotchmarker was renamed the Nel-Spot 007 when produced and marketed by Nelson in 1972. By this time, paintballs were not just being used to mark trees but also cattle.

In 1993 Daisy joined Canadian paintball company Brass Eagle in manufacturing paintball markers for the recreational sports market. Two years later, Daisy acquired Brass Eagle, and in 1997 Brass Eagle was separated from Daisy via a public stock offering.

Winchester Air Rifles

In September 2000 Daisy was approached by the recently retired President of Browning firearms, Don Gobel, who was working on special projects for their company. Olin Corporation owns the rights to the Winchester® brand. Browning licenses the brand for the production of firearms. Both Olin and Browning were interested in having a leading airgun company apply the Winchester brand to create a line of quality air rifles.

The two brands were a natural fit. The agreement was attractive to Daisy because of Winchester's superior brand recognition and quality reputation in the firearm category. Daisy believed that a line of Winchester Air Rifles would provide an assortment of guns with high-end features and immediate brand recognition and appeal. Olin and Browning recognized that Daisy was the airgun category leader and that the company would be quickly successful in placing Winchester Air Rifles with major retailers.

At an industry convention in early 2001 Daisy unveiled a line of break barrel, .177 caliber and .22 caliber pellet air rifles under the Winchester Air Rifle brand. Following Mr. Gobel's retirement, the company has continued to enjoy successful placement of product and an excellent relationship with its partners at Browning and Olin Corporation for over ten years.

First Nature,
a Division of Daisy Outdoor Products

Before Ray Hobbs joined Daisy, he had served as Chairman of the Executive Committee for Bass Pro Shops. Prior to that, he had retired from Wal-Mart as Senior Vice President of Merchandising, following twenty-three years with the retailer. Ray also owns a consulting company, D & R Hobbs Business Consulting, through which he consults with a variety of entrepreneurial clients dealing with business startups, expansions and line extensions, licensing, franchising, and branding.

In 2001 Ray was contacted by Grady Fort. The two had known each other when Ray had merchandised hard lines, including birding products, for Wal-Mart and Grady had owned a game feeder company. Grady was interested in marketing a line of birdfeeders.

Both men recognized the huge potential represented by the birding market. Research data at that time consistently indicated that over eighty-five percent of households in the United States reported feeding or watching birds as an outdoor activity. The two discussed product features and price points, and Grady showed Ray some of his unique design concepts which both believed to be patentable.

Grady was interested in partnering with a company with the experience and capability to manufacture and market his products to birding, farm and home and discount stores.

Ray was intrigued by the unique product designs and the sheer magnitude of the birding market. He also recognized that birding sales and airgun sales occur in different, complementary seasons. Ray presented a business plan to Daisy's Board of Directors who approved the creation of a First Nature birding division of Daisy Outdoor Products.

To gauge the potential of the initial designs, the two men presented the concepts to the Wal-Mart Divisional Manager for pet products and the pet products Buyer. Based on their initial positive reaction to the first feeder design and reacting to their constructive suggestions, First Nature, by Daisy, would proceed with production of the first of many successful designs: the Seed Selector. The feeder was easily recognized by its large colorful hopper, which could hold five pounds of seed, and a patented ring, which could be turned to feed either mixed bird seed or thistle seed. Within one year, the Seed Selector was Wal-Mart's number one selling bird feeder.

The First Nature product line was founded on the management team's belief that birding products should equally emphasize function, innovative features, ease of cleaning and attractive design. Soon a hummingbird feeder and nectar concentrate were added to the product line. With a patented two-part base and wide mouth jar this hummingbird feeder was easier to clean than any other feeders on the market. The nectar concentrate contained food-grade sucrose and mixed easily with water.

Feedback from birding buyers indicated that, in order to qualify as a full-line birding supplier, First Nature would need to expand its line to include traditional wooden feeders and bird houses. First Nature acquired the name and assets of Nature's Niche, an existing line of wooden bird houses, bat and ladybug houses

Daisy brand. The efficiency of integrating additional product lines under the expertise of existing personnel and delivery systems remains attractive.

Daisy, today, remains positioned – through start-up, acquisition or line extension – to apply the Daisy brand to other outdoor recreational product categories or foster select new products under the Daisy Outdoor Products corporate umbrella.

and decorative bird feeders. In keeping with the company's effort to support the local community, Daisy sourced the production of the line with a local community college which used the production to teach wood-working skills. While wooden bird houses and feeders are no longer a part of the product line, First Nature seed feeders, hummingbird feeders and nectar concentrate are top category performers for many major retailers.

First Nature, a division of Daisy, is an excellent example of how even a seemingly unrelated business category start-up can offset the seasonality of Daisy's airgun business while benefiting from Daisy's existing infrastructure, capabilities, contacts and retail trade experience.

The Daisy Outdoor Products Umbrella
The launch of a line of pocket knives and rechargeable lights are both additional examples of how the company continues to foray into closely related outdoor recreation product categories by leveraging the strength of the

Chapter 14
It All Starts Here

The Age-Old Question
Which came first, the firearm or the airgun? If you include blowguns in the category of airguns (after all, they're air-powered) then the airgun wins. If you limit the comparison to mechanically energized devices, then the firearm wins as there were Chinese cannons, multi-barreled guns and rockets around 700 A.D..

Certainly, throughout history, airguns have followed trends in firearm technology and design. The Rogers Daisy Airgun Museum houses examples of high-powered large caliber air rifles dating to the seventeenth century which look very much like flintlock rifles.

One thing is certain: for most Americans, their initial experience in the shooting sports was not with a firearm but with a BB gun. Airguns, as a category, represent the front door to the world of shooting sports. An adult who has never shot a BB gun and who did not grow up in a hunting or gun-owning family is much less likely to hunt or get involved in the shooting sports. Because of Daisy's longevity, multi-generational appeal and dominance of the youth airgun subcategory, it is most likely that a person's first airgun is a Daisy BB gun. That's why the company coined the slogan, It All Starts Here.

Because of the Second Amendment right which American's enjoy and because of the American hunting heritage, it would be irresponsible to venture that there would not be a firearms industry today if it were not for Daisy. There is no doubt, however, that the most avid and accomplished hunters and the most talented marksmen will have to confess that they took their first shot with a Daisy.

At the annual National Rifle Association's National Convention, Daisy's customers are there in droves. The most frequent comment of the thousands of NRA members and supporters that all come by the Daisy booth begins with the words, "My first gun was a Daisy."

Firearms did exist before airguns.

Daisy didn't invent the airgun.

However, for firearms advocates, it all started with that first shot from a Daisy BB gun.

On the occasion of the company's 125th anniversary, Daisy asked several of our corporate friends to express, in their own words, how shooting a Daisy affected their lives.

Daisy is humbly aware of and grateful that, for the entire shooting population and industry, it all starts here, with a Daisy BB gun.

Lou Ferrigno Enterprises, Inc.

January 1, 2011

Daisy Outdoor Products
400 West Stribling Drive
Rogers, Arkansas 72756

Dear Friends at Daisy,

While Daisy has now been around for 125 years, my first experience with Daisy BB guns was as a kid back in Brooklyn, where I grew up. I loved to shoot the rifles at the Arcades in Coney Island. Sometimes, I recall, they would also have Daisy BB guns for the youngsters to shoot.

I learned several things from shooting the Daisy BB guns. Firstly, I learned that a BB gun is a great way to concentrate and to focus (especially when I hit the targets and won prizes!) Secondly, I learned the basics of shooting properly. Thirdly, I learned that it's fun to compete against yourself and to improve your skill level.

For several generations, shooters of all ages have enjoyed the fun of shooting Daisy BB guns. For me, shooting with a Daisy was the foundation for learning how to shoot properly.

When my wife and I bought Daisy airguns for my kids to shoot, that instantly brought back all of those wonderful memories of my childhood. Even today, one of my greatest passions is shooting airguns together with my boys!

Let me take this opportunity to congratulate my friends at Daisy on the company's 125th anniversary. Your company has provided a wholesome and rewarding activity for millions and I hope that Daisy will continue to prosper.

Sincerely,

Lou Ferrigno

Lou Ferrigno

621 17th St. • Santa Monica, California 90402 • Telephone 310/395-2144 Fax 310/395-6605
carlamay1@aol.com

NATIONAL RIFLE ASSOCIATION OF AMERICA
11250 WAPLES MILL ROAD
FAIRFAX, VIRGINIA 22030

WAYNE LAPIERRE
Executive Vice President

Dear Daisy Family:

"My first gun … was a Daisy."

Each year at the NRA Annual Meetings I have the pleasure of standing next to my friends in the Daisy Outdoor Products booth, and every year that is routinely the first line I hear from all in attendance. Not because it's some marketing-speak market-goers felt obliged to express. Or that's what a freedom-loving American thought I needed to hear.

Hardly.

It's a genuine, heart-felt celebration. Something that when said, immediately transports each person back to that perfect day: as a child, the owner of that new, precious BB gun. Holding your first Daisy has been an important rite of passage in millions of families. With each new airgun, we teach our children about firearm freedoms, and the responsibilities that go with them. In turn, they bequeath those same values—a cycle represented by the hundreds of Daisy models over decades of careful, devoted production.

From hosting postal matches, to their tireless support of organizations like 4-H, The American Legion, JROTC, the U.S. Jaycees and the Boy Scouts of America, the NRA honors—and is in awe of—Daisy's 125 years of success. And we anticipate the generations to come, those who will wistfully reminisce and proudly say …"My first gun … was a Daisy."

Yours in Freedom (and Fun),

Wayne LaPierre

Wayne LaPierre
Executive Vice President
National Rifle Association

(703) 267-1020
(703) 267-3989 fax
wlapierre@nrahq.org

PETER BILLINGSLEY
Los Angeles, California

December 23, 2010

Joe C. Murfin
V.P. Marketing
Daisy Outdoor Products
400 West Stribling Drive
Rogers, AR 72756

Dear Joe,

In many ways it's hard to imagine my life without the influence of Daisy. When I was nine years old my brother received a Daisy Pal for Christmas. My envy overwhelming, he generously allowed it to become "our" air rifle. And there in the open spaces of Arizona first began my long and rewarding relationship with shooting.

The small rifle made of wood and blue steel didn't just teach me how to aim and pull a trigger, it taught me a responsibility and gave me a confidence, which has carried over today into my love of shooting pistols and sporting clays.

A couple of years after first holding that Daisy Pal, I received another Daisy gun. This time it was a Red Ryder carbine-action 200-shot range-model air rifle.   It was given to me by Bob Clark who had just directed me in a small film called, "A Christmas Story." Little did I know in that moment just how indelible my relationship with the Red Ryder would become.

Congratulations Daisy, on one hundred and twenty-five years of bringing such joy to so many. I have no doubt it's only the beginning.

Sincerely,

Peter Billingsley

Nancy Napolski Johnson

Dear Daisy—

As I look back through the years of my involvement in the shooting sports, a smile comes to my face when I think of my humble beginnings. It was in the very beginning that I shot a Daisy (pump action) air rifle out my kitchen window, my brother by my side, steadying my shaky hold. I did not go on to compete with a Daisy, but it was with a Daisy I got my start. It was a Daisy air rifle that helped lay the foundation for my future in the shooting sports.

Many years later, many years removed from my Olympic victory in Sydney, I can still look back and remember how I got my start in the shooting sports. Had it not been for Daisy Manufacturing, I'm not sure there would have been an Olympic Gold medal in my future. Daisy is responsible for introducing and educating millions of shooters worldwide. As the oldest and largest manufacturer of air guns, Daisy remains a backbone of the shooting industry. Their dedication to the shooting sports resounds in so many of our youth who get their start with a Daisy. Through the manufacturing and supply of an amazing line of air guns, they are giving people an affordable means to break into the shooting sports.

On my first trip to the Daisy factory, I had the privilege of building my own Daisy air rifle, which I excitedly gave to my four-year-old daughter. It will mean so much to know we both fired our first shots from a Daisy.

Thank you, Daisy for all that you have done for the shooting sports!

Your friend-

Nancy Napolski Johnson
2000 Olympic Gold Medalist

Governor Mike Huckabee

January 18, 2011

Dear Fellow Daisy BB Gun Owners:

For 125 years, the Daisy brand has been the gold standard for air guns and like most of us who become firearms enthusiasts and hunters, it all started with a Daisy BB gun. It certainly did for me.

As a young boy in south Arkansas, I got a Daisy Model 25 for Christmas. My Dad was adamant that I operate that BB gun with all the safety concerns as if it were a .300 caliber rifle, but it was the way that most of us learned how to handle and respect a firearm.

Hours and hours were spent with my Daisy BB gun, mostly shooting tin cans set on fence posts. But the basic lessons of shooting etiquette were learned with that BB gun. Later when I would get my first pellet gun and later a .22 rifle, it was the fundamentals learned from using the Daisy BB gun that would form the foundation for my gun ethics.

I still have that BB gun, and it's in pristine condition and I consider it one of my genuine treasures. The very sight of it brings warm and nostalgic feelings of days long gone when boys learned to be men. Daisy was a big part of that transition for many of us.

Sincerely,

Mike Huckabee

Mike Huckabee

P. O. Box 2008   Little Rock, AR 72203
            501-324-2008

The Roy Rogers-Dale Evans Museum & Happy Trails Theater
3950 Green Mountain Drive
Branson, MO 65616

December 8th, 2010

Joe Murfin
V.P. Of Marketing Daisy
PO Box 220
Rogers, AR. 72757

Dear Mr. Murfin,

What a great milestone! 125 years - congratulations! That's the cowboy way!

My 1st gun was a cap pistol with my Fathers name on it – A Roy Rogers cap pistol – and I wore it constantly. When I was 7 years old, my father bought me a Daisy BB Gun. Nothin' fancy, just a good ol' gun. He taught my brother Sandy and I several lessons with that little rifle. First of all and most important, how to handle a gun safely. Secondly how to conserve those precious BB's. He would only put in one cap full of BB's from the Daisy BB tube into our guns. Then he would teach us accuracy by placing ping pong balls on top of empty pop bottles. We had to learn to shoot the ball off without breaking the bottle. After all, the pop bottle was worth 5¢ deposit that we could cash in and buy candy bars and gum!

It was my most prized possession that Daisy air rifle. It's hard to believe that gun has been around for 125 years. Let's pray for another 125 years – the kids of America need Daisy!

Happy Trails To You All!

Roy Rogers Jr.

Roy Rogers Jr.
Dusty

Phone: 417-339-1900 • Fax: 417-339-2307 • www.royrogers.com
Museum and Gift Shop open daily 9:00 a.m. – 6:00 p.m.
Happy Trails Theater: Shows Tuesday – Saturday 10:00 a.m. & 2:00 p.m. thru mid-Dec.

STEPHEN A. WOMACK
THIRD DISTRICT, ARKANSAS

E-MAIL — womack@mail.house.gov
WEBSITE — womack.house.gov

Congress of the United States
House of Representatives
Washington, DC 20515-0403

HOUSE APPROPRIATIONS COMMITTEE
SUBCOMMITTEE ON TRANSPORTATION, HOUSING AND URBAN DEVELOPMENT, AND RELATED AGENCIES

SUBCOMMITTEE ON
ENERGY AND WATER DEVELOPMENT

SUBCOMMITTEE ON
FINANCIAL SERVICES AND GENERAL GOVERNMENT

To my friends at Daisy:

Congratulations on the occasion of your 125th Birthday!

As I reflect on the impact Daisy Manufacturing has had on me personally and professionally, I am consumed by fond memories—as a child, veteran, and public official.

Like millions of other men and women, I will always remember the days of my youth spent in the yard taking aim at cans, bottles, and milk cartons—the stationary targets of choice—and the occasional "moving" target that might land nearby.

Little did I know at the time that the skills developed by perfecting my stance, aim, breathing, grip, etc. would play such a valuable role in my 30-year service in the Army National Guard. Basic rifle marksmanship seemed to always come easy for me given my experience with my trusted Daisy air rifle. And, I was always proud to know that the precision guns used to teach marksmanship to the officer candidates at the University of Arkansas ROTC program were Daisys.

There is no better source of pride, however, than to have presided as mayor over the city Daisy calls home. From its move to Rogers in 1958, the tribute to Cass Hough and the Daisy centennial in 1986, to the return of its manufacturing operations in 2007, the citizens of Rogers have always valued the close association with its beloved industrial cornerstone. It's why the preferred gift to a visiting dignitary is a Daisy air rifle.

More than anything, however, I have truly appreciated the leadership of Daisy employees. Everywhere you turn, Daisy employees and their families are investing in their communities. Our schools, churches, civic and non-profit organizations, hospital, local government, and other valued institutions have prospered from Daisy leadership.

Many thanks for valuable contributions to Rogers, our state, and the nation. Best wishes for a continued prosperous future.

Warm Regards,

Steve Womack
Member of Congress

WASHINGTON DC
1508 LONGWORTH HOUSE OFFICE BUILDING
WASHINGTON, DC 20515
(202) 225-4301

ROGERS
3333 PINNACLE HILLS PARKWAY, #120
ROGERS, AR 72758
(479) 464-0446

FORT SMITH
423 NORTH 6TH STREET
FORT SMITH, AR 72902
(479) 424-1146

HARRISON
303 NORTH MAIN STREET, SUITE 102
HARRISON, AR 72601
(870) 741-6900

PRINTED ON RECYCLED PAPER

JOHN BOOZMAN
ARKANSAS

United States Senate
WASHINGTON, DC 20510

March 11, 2011

Daisy Outdoor Products
PO Box 220
Rogers, AR 72757-0220

Dear Friends at Daisy,

Congratulations on the 125th Anniversary of Daisy Outdoor Products! I am honored to be part of your anniversary celebration and for the opportunity to contribute to this book honoring the Daisy family.

A favorite Christmas memory is when I was about ten years old and received my Daisy Red Ryder BB Gun. I had wanted one for a long time. I had great fun and literally wore it out with my friends.

I was so pleased recently to welcome Daisy Outdoor Products back to my hometown in Rogers. Daisy is important not only in our local area, but throughout Arkansas and beyond. Your leadership and dedication to all who enjoy target shooting sets the standard.

I especially appreciate the support Daisy gives to youth programs, such as the 4-H Shooting Sports Program and to the Boy Scouts. These are invaluable to young people and have served as the safety standard from one generation to another. Many small and large game hunters, professional shooters, and recreational shooters, began with a Daisy air rifle. They learned the basics of gun safety and marksmanship, and developed a life-long appreciation for the shooting sports because of your legacy.

Again, congratulations on your 125th Anniversary! I wish you continued success in the future.

Sincerely,

John Boozman

John Boozman
U.S. Senator

JB: kg

Postscript
Passing the Baton

Cass Hough's book *It's a Daisy!* spans the first ninety years of the company's history. At the close of his book, in a chapter entitled "Daisy Can Do It Again," he quotes the poem "Grandfather Squeers," penned by his father's favorite poet, James Whitcomb Riley. I'm familiar with the poet and poem because my late father, a Hoosier himself, had collected the entire works of Riley. In "Grandfather Squeers," the old man, having achieved his ninetieth birthday, stated, "I've the hang of it now and can do it again."

None of us mortals have the opportunity to repeat our performance. Rather, we celebrate our accomplishments, learn from our mistakes and benefit from both.

We, today's Daisy team, take seriously the charge to preserve, protect and promote this great old brand. Most of what we're protecting today, we've inherited – a rich heritage of 125 years. We're constantly reminded of the fact that our history is long, our future is bright and we're only here for a moment in the middle of that continuum.

How can we ensure preservation of these things we hold dear?

In 2004, at the Athens Olympic Games, both the United States' men's and women's 100-meter relay teams failed to win the Gold, not due to the speed of any one runner but due to a baton exchange not made within the zone. Many of us have long forgotten the details of running a relay race in high school. A relay team is comprised of four runners, each running a leg of the race and carrying a baton which must be passed to the next runner. Some say that it's important to save your best runner to run the last leg of the race, so they know what it takes to win the race. But the truth is each runner can run their best time and the race can still be lost by the failure to exchange the baton within the exchange zone.

If we are to preserve our heritage for the future, we'd better be building our relay team. This race will not be completed in our lifetime. We're just living one leg of the race. How we run the race is certainly important, but that we hand off the baton well is even more important. That will ensure our legacy.

We're proud to be on the Daisy team today, working to preserve, for future generations, everything for which Daisy stands. We've run a great race. We'll leave a great legacy. Soon, we must hand off our baton to future generations who will love, guard, protect and promote this great Daisy heritage for another 125 years.

Trademark Acknowledgment

Corporate names and brand names which appear in this book, including AC Spark Plug Division, Square D Manufacturing Company, Palmer-Bee Company, Ligon Brothers, Bendix Aviation, Nippert Electric Company, Pilgrim Drawn Steel Corporation, Murchison Brothers, Victor Comptometer, 1903 A3 Springfield, Avedis Zildjian Cymbal Company, Red Ryder, Warner Home Video, Burke Golf Equipment Corporation, PGA Golf, Worthington Ball Company, Ertl Toys, Valley Manufacturing and Sales, Nissen Gymnastics, Bear Archery, Kidde & Company, Hanson Industries/Hanson Trust, Stephens Inc., Charter Oak Partners, Sundblom Studios, John Q. Hammons Convention Center, D'Arcy Advertising, Coca-Cola, Borden's Milk, 7 Up, the Art Institute of Chicago, All Metal Products Company, Sears Roebuck & Company, James Heddon's Sons Company, Open Avenues, The Benton County Sunshine School, Arkansas Children's Hospital, United Way of Manhattan, United Way of Northwest Arkansas, Rebuilding Together of Northwest Arkansas, Arkansas Governor's Workplace Award, Malcolm Baldrige Criteria, Airgun Digest, American Alliance for Health, Physical Education and Recreation, University of Michigan, Junior Chambers (Jaycees), 4-H Shooting Sports, American Legion, the National Rifle Association of America, National Guard Youth Marksmanship Program, USA Shooting, Cadet Leagues of Canada, Royal Rangers, the International Hunter Education Association, Youth Shooting Sports Alliance, the American Society for Testing Materials, The Consumer Product Safety Commission, National Electronic Injury Surveillance System, Locker Greenberg & Brainin, P.C., Arkansas & Missouri Railroad, D & R Hobbs Properties, LLC, D & R Hobbs Business Consulting, Nabholtz Construction Company, Ken's Signs, Southwest Power and Electric, Rodden Landscaping, Rescue Heroes and Crossland Construction, BEI Electric, Rogers Iron and Metal, Moser Furniture Company, Hunter Ceiling Fans, Wal-Mart, Iver Johnson, Nelson Paint Company, Brass Eagle, Winchester, Browning, Olin Corp., the Olympic Games are all names which are, like the Daisy-owned brands mentioned in this book, registered trademarks of their respective owners.